My Life as a Sidekick to Heroes

"Tony" "Best thing that happened for Riverwoods"
your friend
Herde

My Life as a Sidekick to Heroes

What Will Your Legacy Be?

by
Harold Jerde

xulon PRESS

"My Life as a Sidekick to Heroes is not only an interesting read, but very inspiring. The amazing stories motivated me to do more for God's kingdom. As you read how God has used ordinary people to make a difference in the lives of others, you begin to see how God can use anyone to change the world. It only takes a willing heart. The book made it very clear that Harold is not only the sidekick; he is indeed one of God's exceptional heroes."

Shirley Rose
Executive Producer/Host, "Aspiring Women"
Total Living Network

"Harold's life, as you can read about in these memoirs, is proof that one person can make a difference. See a need. Do what you can in Jesus' name to help. Move on to the next need. Could life be any simpler, any more satisfying, any more rewarding, any more complete?"

Levern Halstead
Founder/Director
Farsight Christian Mission

"Harold challenges each of us to answer the question—what am I willing to accept to lead others to Christ? I know his answer. 'Whatever it takes.'"

Bill Mills
Former President
Christian Appalachian Project

"It has been an amazing adventure to watch the Lord work in the lives of many people. It is my prayer that after reading this book you will also have an urgency to serve the Lord by serving those in need."

Kyle J. Martin, age 22
Harold's "Youngest Best Friend"

"Going on a mission trip with Harold is an experience you will never forget. He is a cheerful leader. He loves serving the Lord every day the Lord gives him."

Tim Sheldon
Circuit Court Judge
Kane County, Illinois

"Be careful as you read what follows. You're going to get hooked. And then you're not going to be content until you, too, get on board with the mission of proclaiming Christ far and wide."

Dr. James L. Nicodem
Senior Pastor
Christ Community Church

Dedication

To Carol, my wife of fifty-six years, and to my family.

Table of Contents

✧

Acknowledgments

Many thanks to my editor and true friend, Rose Dally, who has witnessed mission work. To Tony Pecoraro, my friend and traveler on many mission trips, for arranging the book and setting up the pictures. To Debbie Cole, my friend who has also traveled on many mission trips, for the final edit.

Paul Campbell has been a wonderful friend to me. He has been the most helpful person behind all I do. He volunteers to work for me when I am on mission trips. He doesn't go on mission trips, but his mission is to help me so I can go. When I'm home, he volunteers to help me as I work with nonprofit organizations. We work together so often that many times, when I plan to work on a project, people ask, "Is Paul coming with you?" We can get much more work done together than most teams. Paul knows how I work, and I know how he works, often making it almost unnecessary for us to even talk about the job as we work. Paul uses his own machinery and gives of his time to help others almost every day. Thanks, Paul. You are a friend like no other and one of my heroes!

Preface

O ver the past forty years of my life God has continued to impress on my heart the practical applications of the Scripture verse found in Matthew 5:13: "You are the salt of the earth." Salt has been used in the past for preservation as well as for seasoning. I am convinced we have been called to act as salt and positively influence the lives of others.

God has definite plans for our lives as devoted followers of Christ. At times over the years I have not been certain where God is leading me or where He is leading those who ask for my input for direction in their lives. Time after time I have seen God direct people who willingly volunteer to serve others without expecting to receive anything in return. Often, amazingly, God opens doors and directs hearts into His plan for their next steps or life calling. I am convinced that being available to God, others and opportunities meets needs for those being served and for those serving. Rather than our expecting fulfillment from others, possessions and positive circumstances, I suggest we seek fulfillment through investing ourselves in others, bringing hope and help to their hurting lives.

As I have followed God through the doors He has opened for me, I have met many unsung heroes who have inspired, encouraged and worked alongside me. This book includes some of their stories as well as my personal observations and comments others have termed "Haroldisms." I pray that each reader will be spurred on to actions of love and good works among the needy God puts in their path. Blessings will be returned to you and in turn be passed on to others. Everywhere I go I find new friends. The connections we make together just help more of the Lord's work get done.

In God's service our greatest service ability is our availability.

Harold Jerde

Chapter 1

The Early Years

As I begin this book, I thank God for the many people I have met who are serving the Lord. Some of these people I met through intentional visits to mission stations or during planned visits to support missionaries in places like Barbados, Mexico, Costa Rica, Jamaica, Czech Republic, Haiti, Brazil, Alaska and Kentucky. Sometimes I have met people "accidentally" when the Lord simply put them in my path. I am amazed how many interesting people and stories there are to write about, and I am thankful for the privilege of passing these stories on to you. Some of the stories are written directly by those who lived them; others I will tell in my own words.

In the 1970s on my first mission trip to Brazil I thought maybe someday, when I was fifty-five years old, I would be involved in ministries such as these. But when I reached fifty-five I was financially stable enough so I never had to work another day as long as I lived and my mind was no longer thinking of mission work. The Lord, however, had other plans for me. I had to lose most of my financial security before I returned to searching out the plans He had for me.

I guess the plans the Lord had for me began a long while before my adult years. I grew up in a Christian family, attended a very conservative Lutheran church and went to Sunday school from an early age and had fifteen years of perfect attendance.

One thing I loved about my family while I was growing up was that we always had fun with my uncles and their friends. I spent a lot of time with six uncles on my mother's side especially. I always hung around older people and ended up with the nickname Timer, short for old-timer.

I was given a second nickname. I used to hang out at my uncle's gas station, and one day the postman stopped by and asked my name. I kind of mumbled and said "Harold" softly. My uncle said, "Say Harold plain!" So I repeated, "Harold Plain." After that my uncles called me Harold Plain.

I loved the stories my family told, and to this day I especially like sayings and quotes. I am known for repeating these sayings and quotes as well as coming up with some of my own. These sayings are now called "Haroldisms"—if there is such a word.

One thing I miss the most, though, is the good time of just visiting people and hearing the stories of friends, relatives or even strangers. At our family reunions fifty to seventy-five people would show up every year. Our Halverson-Hendrickson reunions were held in Morris, Illinois, one year and De Kalb, Illinois, the next year. Both sides of our family came from Norway, many of them settling in the village of Norway, Illinois. Now I do my best to meet people in restaurants and coffee shops when I am not on mission trips or working.

While I was a young boy, our home was like Grand Central Station with someone always coming or going. My mother would get up in the morning and put a pot of coffee on the stove, and in the people would come.

When I came home from school, my mother was there waiting for me except during the years of World War II. At that time many of the women worked in factories, and my mother was an example of what they called a "Rosie the Riveter" in war defense posters. Mother built radio shelters for communications at the nearby factory which had been converted from a wagon works business. My friends and I would walk down to the factory after school and stand by the outside window and talk to her for a few minutes.

I also remember after the war was over, when I came home for lunch at noon, a "bum," now called a homeless person, would often be sitting on our back steps eating a meal my mother had made for him. My ma, as we called her, was a "mark," which meant if a bum received a good meal at a home, he would make a mark on the curb so his fellow bums could see where they could get a good meal.

I lived in this station for the first six years of my life.
This is Dad in the picture.

Our home was located only three blocks from the railroad. About six blocks from our house was the Del Monte packing factory where corn, peas and beans were packed and shipped. During World War II German prisoners from the camp at Rockford were hauled in open trucks to work at that canning factory. Many of the prisoners were about fifteen to twenty years old. My friends and I would throw packages of cigarettes to them as the trucks passed by us on the road. (Shame on us!) Cigarettes cost thirteen cents a pack at that time, and even I had that much money. We would wave and have a lot of fun with them, as most of the prisoners were not too much older than we were.

I do not remember the pipe.

I was recently reminiscing about the simple life we had when I was in school. I began first grade in 1938. At that time we did not have kindergarten or many of the materials students today take for granted such as ball point pens, calculators, computers, cell phones or radios with head phones. Grownups did not need to organize our ball games. Then I had never heard of playing soccer. To this day I don't understand the game and do not enjoy watching it. I must be an old-timer, but I believe our growing up during those years was more fundamental than all the abundance of what kids have and need to put up with today. Other things we had then that are not around anymore include Blackjack chewing gum, candy ciga-rettes, home milk delivery in glass bottles with cardboard stoppers, party-line telephones, newsreels at the theater before movies, PF Flyers, Butch Wax, TV test patterns, peashooters, Howdy Doody, 45 rpm records, S&H Green stamps, hi-fis, blue flashbulbs, Packard or Studebaker automobiles, roller-skate keys, cork pop guns, drive-in movies, wash tub wringers, to mention a few. We sure don't need them anymore, I guess.

From the time I was in fifth grade I had at least two jobs. I would get up every morning to haul milk into town from the farms in our area. Then I would go to school and come home at 3:30. In the winter when I got home from school a truck full of coal would be waiting for me to unload because my dad hauled coal for his trucking busi-ness. Even though I was small it would be my job to push the coal out of the truck into a basement coal bin.

On Saturdays I had a third butter-and-egg job. My best friend was about eighteen years older than I was. He had a business of picking up butter and eggs from the local farmers during the week. On Saturdays I would go with him when he drove the butter and eggs into the city of Chicago and peddled them to homes and businesses on his route. Then we would bring back a load of soda pop to sell to the farmers. At that time no "bad guys" were around to bother us, and going into Chicago was much like going downtown in our little hometown. This butter-and-egg business continued for a few years.

One of the families we sold eggs to had a daughter my friend fell in love with. After about a year or so my friend didn't ask me to go with him anymore. My friend and the girl got married. I've often kidded her and told her I never really cared for her since she ruined my butter-and-egg job and took away the fun time of going to Chicago with my best friend. We've laughed together about this. We remained close to them and visited them often during the years their family was growing to include children. We continue our relationship even now as my wife and I manage an apartment building for these friends.

We always called my father Daddy. One of the things I remember most about him was that he was always talking to someone about the Lord. For that very reason unsaved people didn't want to hang out with him much, but if they ever found themselves in trouble they knew his phone number. Daddy was a lay pastor in the Lutheran church. He would travel around to different towns to help out pastors who needed a break. Every Sunday after church he hosted a radio program at our local station, WLBK, in De Kalb, Illinois. My father started a string band at our church. They often traveled to other towns in our area. Daddy was also the president of the Norwegian Intermission Society which held tent meetings in the surrounding towns during the summer. During these tent meetings the Holy Spirit would be at work convicting people of their sin. They would walk down the aisle, crying and repenting of their sin.

When we first moved into De Kalb, my dad worked at American Steel where they made barbed wire. Barbed wire was reported to be invented in De Kalb, so De Kalb has been nicknamed Barb City. After being employed at American Steel Daddy worked in the trucking and concrete block business. I still meet people who tell me he was their Sunday school teacher and how much they miss him.

When I was in grade school and Daddy was involved in mission outreaches, he would often volunteer to drive the visiting missionary or evangelist to the train or bus station for their trip home, frequently to Minnesota or Wisconsin. When they got to the station my father asked them if they had money to buy their ticket home. Many times they said no, and my dad would give them the money they needed. I continue to be amazed at the faith of these missionaries and evangelists who knew the Lord would take care of their every need, even though they did not have what they needed at the time as they traveled wherever they were called. One of the most important things Daddy taught us was to help whomever we could.

Another memory I have of my dad is when he heard something he thought was funny, he would laugh until he cried. Once he started laughing it was hard for him to stop. When I was younger I was much the same, though now I can control it better.

When I was nineteen years old I was attending school in Minneapolis, Minnesota. I came home at Christmastime and received an "invitation" to join the army. This was during the Korean War and the military draft. I decided I would rather ride for four years than walk for two years; this resulted in my decision to join the Air Force at the same time several of my friends enlisted.

While I was in the Air Force I got married. My wife, Carol, and I had two children before I was discharged.

After completing my tour of duty in the military, I came back home to De Kalb and worked with my dad in the trucking business. I worked in concrete block manufacturing for a short time before returning to school. School did not last long, because I decided I wanted to get into the building business and real estate. I did very well professionally. My wife was also employed, and financially things were going great.

Before I go further in my story I want to tell you how I met my wife, Carol. Throughout the fifty-six years we have been together I've kidded her about how she came all the way from Thief River Falls to get me. People used to talk about how far Thief River Falls was located up in northern Minnesota. My mother used to say, "It's not the end of the world, but you can see the end from there."

My mother met Carol before I did. I say ours was an arranged marriage because my mother was a fixer-upper. Carol had come to De Kalb to be in her sister's wedding. Mother attended the wedding and invited Carol, Carol's sister and her new husband from De Kalb over to our home for dinner. Through connections good things seem to take place in my life.

Carol decided to stay in De Kalb and started sewing for a company that made coats. She came from a large family with fourteen children, learned to make all her own dresses and had to share everything she had with her siblings. Because she knew how to sew she was prepared to work for the coat company. This was also how she helped support our family while I went to school for a short time. When I got into the home building business, Carol painted the houses after they were built. I have been so lucky that she has been a helper in all we have ever done. She still helps me manage a sixteen-unit apartment building. Carol has gone with me on some of my mission trips to other countries and within the United States.

When I talk to my friends who are thinking of getting married, I tell them not to marry until they can't wait to see their girlfriend when they get off work at the end of the day. That's the way it is with me. When I'm on my way home from wherever I go, I can't wait to see my lady!

I had always been active in our church, but I was not a true believer and knew I should be making changes in my life. Our family went to church every Sunday morning, Sunday evening and for midweek services; but we still did not know the Lord personally, and we didn't know what He wanted to do in our lives.

An evangelist was preaching at our church in the mid 1950s, and he joined us at my parents' home for coffee one evening after the evangelistic meetings. He asked my wife if we were saved. She gave an honest answer and said no. Then he asked if he could come to our home the next night, and she agreed that would be fine. I could have pinched her. I knew the walk, and I knew the talk; but I wasn't interested in living my life that way. I remembered the words, however, to a song we used to sing: "Have you counted the cost if your soul should be lost. . . ?" That song goes on to say, "There is a line that is drawn for rejecting the Lord, and the call of the Lord comes no more. . . . Even now it may be that the line you have crossed. . . . Have you counted, have you counted the cost?" (A.J. Hodge, copyright 1923, renewed 1951, Word Music Inc.).

I didn't expect the Lord to continue to call forever, so on that night in 1956 my wife and I both counted the cost. I have been a Christian since that night but made a decision to be a devoted follower of Jesus about twenty years ago when I knew I wanted to work for the Lord. I believe the Lord has a plan for everyone's life. If the plan for your life isn't working, then go help someone else with their plan until you discover how your life plan will come to be.

This is a picture of our family: Carol and I are in the middle, our daughter, son-in-law and three granddaughters are to our right. Our oldest son, daughter-in-law, grandson and granddaughter are at the top right. On the left is our youngest son, his wife and two children.

Top left: Darin Jerde, Allison Jerde, Krista Jerde, Eric Jerde, Donna Jerde, Danny Jerde and Allison Smith. Second row: Hanna Jerde, Elsa Jerde, Carol Jerde, Harold Jerde, Debbie Smith, John Smith. Front row: Natalie Smith, Danielle Smith.

Chapter 2

Making Connections and Reaching Out

Brazil

As I mentioned earlier I grew up in a very conservative Lutheran church where the Word of God was preached. Missionaries frequently visited our congregation. One of these missionaries, John Abel, served on a mission field in Brazil. John impressed me during one of his visits in the early 1970s, so I told him I would travel to Brazil to see his work firsthand. He ministered by holding tent meetings sharing the gospel in small villages around his base in Compo Mourao, Brazil.

As long as I was planning a trip to Brazil, I decided to connect with another friend, a new missionary to Brazil, who was from my wife's hometown. I wrote the friend a letter, sending it to him at his language school in San Paulo, and told him I was coming for a visit on my way to Compo Mourao. As it happened, he never received my letter; it was returned to me at home in De Kalb three months later. I had his address in San Paulo, so I was able to find him for what was now a surprise visit. He was then able to connect me by telephone with John Abel four hundred miles away in Compo Mourao, who was also surprised by my visit. When I reached Compo Mourao I helped John put up the tent for the next tent meeting. Then we went to a sawmill in the area and borrowed some wooden planks to use for benches for the people to sit on.

Across the street from where we pitched the large tent lived a lady who would not come to the tent meetings, but she wanted to cook a meal for us. She started a fire in her little rock stove about 10 a.m. When the stove became very hot she put in her loaves of bread to bake as part of our meal. The delicious smell reminded me of my grandma's homemade bread, and it tasted just as good too.

People may not always want to be involved in the ministry outreach you provide for them, but it is important to meet them where they are and use whatever opportunity God opens for conversation with them. I try to use any opportunity given to talk with people about their needs and about the Lord no matter where I am or for what purpose I find myself in their environment.

When it was time to move on to another village I helped take the tent down. We would then set up the tent in our next location. While in this area of Brazil I learned that if you wanted to build a church the city government would give you an allotted piece of land on which to build. This town in which the main mission station was located was only ten years old at the time and already had a population of thirty thousand people. In addition to the church, the missionaries were starting a Bible school that is still doing well today.

John Abel was a teacher in a regular school in Brazil for a few years, but he decided to return to being a missionary even though he earned less money. I am so amazed that missionaries often give up so much to work for the Lord. Only they realize the true blessings that are a part of the Lord's work. Thank you, John, for the time you give working for the Lord!

Ever since I was discharged from the Air Force in 1956 I was in business for myself, building homes, apartments, subdivisions and mobile home parks. I built fourteen condominiums in St. Charles, Illinois, and nine in Batavia. Since much of my building business was located in St. Charles, we decided to move there.

At this time, however, the condo-building business took a downturn; money was plentiful, and people could afford to buy single-family homes rather than condominiums.

Brazil tent meeting during my
very first mission trip in 1971

Because we now lived in St. Charles, someone I worked with recommended a church in the area so I wouldn't have to keep driving back to De Kalb for church. I started attending Christ Community Church where they emphasized getting to know the people around you, making friends and using opportunities with these friends and acquaintances to share about your relationship with the Lord. I thought to myself, "I can do that." The mission of Christ Community Church was, "To know Christ and make Him known." They taught the six Gs: grace, growth, groups, gifts, giving and go. They said to try it, and I would like it. I tried it, and to this day I love it!

Some time earlier I had met a man named Fred Schramm, now owner of Schramm Construction Inc., when he was working for another contractor and I was in the excavation business. I decided to invite Fred and his wife, Annette, to come to a Christmas play at our church. They have attended Christ Community Church ever since.

One day a Haitian missionary visited our church. After the service Fred asked the missionary out for lunch; he was very interested in what this missionary was doing in his hometown in Haiti.

When Fred got home from lunch, he called me to say he was coming over to my house to tell me about the missionary's project. After hearing what Fred had to tell me about Haiti, I said, "Let's go." So together we took a trip to Haiti to see what needed to be done. We found the current stage of the mission project involved in building a second floor on a school. After some preliminary planning we returned home, assembled a team of twenty-one men then returned to Haiti and built a second floor for that school. God enabled me then to make an important connection that would help us carry on additional ministry at a later time. This story will follow later.

That's when I got the bug for mission trips and the Lord's work. I was sixty-five then and began leading mission trips two years later. Boy, am I a late bloomer! I don't want to think about all the wasted years. One of the main reasons I'm writing this book is to get people thinking about what they can do for the Lord. Whatever your age may be, get started now! Fred has become one of my heroes. Thank you, Fred and Annette!

* * *

Fred Schramm's Story

I met Harold while working as a construction superintendent in a suburb of Chicago, Illinois. Harold was always quick to respond and help with tasks that were not included in his scope of work. At the time we met, Harold and his crews were installing the site utilities (storm sewer, sanitary sewer and water mains) on two schools—one junior high and one elementary.

Harold immediately befriended me much as he does everyone he meets, and his intentions were well beyond immediate since he is always thinking of eternity. I had no idea what role he would play in my life. He never gave up on me; he pursued me and my eternal life ignoring my arrogant sinful nature. Often he would say to me, "You need the Lord in your life." My ears were not deaf to his observations of my life. I knew my life was missing something. Each of us has a God-sized hole that only God can fill.

Harold invited me to a men's breakfast one Saturday morning that was hosted by Christ Community Church in St. Charles. A retired air force general delivered the message. It was great! I could not wait to tell my wife about it and asked if we could attend Christ Community the next morning since the same speaker would be delivering the Sunday message. Annette agreed to go, and that started our new life at Christ Community and a journey in a new relationship with Christ in our lives. That was in 1990 or thereabout.

Harold and I have done many things together, but one of the most memorable and impacting things was a trip to Haiti in 1997 to look for a project for a work team. Christ Community had not yet been involved in international ministries. A Haitian pastor who had attended a college here in the western suburbs was being recognized at one of our Sunday services. Christ Community Church had sponsored this young man and helped to pay his college tuition. The pastor spoke of Haiti and the desperate needs they had. Something touched my heart that morning, but I was not the only one.

After the service Harold and I knew we must go for a short trip to Haiti, check out the project and return with a work crew. We did exactly that. We returned with twenty-one men to construct a second level on a small school for the children in Pignon, Haiti. Since then there have been many trips, and Harold has continued with his heart for missions traveling frequently to help those less fortunate in all parts of the world.

My life has changed because of Harold. I am thankful for him and feel so fortunate to call him friend. When I close my eyes and think of Harold I see a man full of joy ready to serve the Lord and others. He has told me to be ready at a moment's notice to be taken to heaven up yonder—in his words, "Always have your bags packed."

I would be remiss if I did not mention one other thing. Behind every good man is a better woman. I know this personally for myself, but Harold has been blessed with his wife, Carol, who is always there supporting him.

Harold, thank you for being my best friend unconditionally.

* * *

Czech Republic

Before I began leading mission trips myself, I went with Christ Community Church on a trip to the Czech Republic. The project we went to work on had been an old communist hideaway. After the fall of communism, buildings became the property of the nearest city or town. The city was then free to use it or sell it. An organization bought this building and used it to teach pastors and missionaries from all of Eastern Europe. The quarters became too small, so our team went to work on adding a third floor onto the existing building. The third floor was to be used as a study and additional living quarters. We worked with a general contractor from the Czech Republic.

While I was there working, I added another member to my list of heroes. His name is Curt Meredith, and he was my roomy for this trip. One night I woke up in the middle of the night to find him sitting on the side of his bed, unable to sleep. I offered to pray with him, and he mentioned he was to give his testimony to the group in the morning. I guessed that was what was bothering him at the time. The next morning Curt gave his testimony of what the Lord had done for him.

Years later he was diagnosed with stage four cancer of the throat, which put him out of commission for a long, long time. He has been close to death a couple of times and was in pain month after month. He put his trust in the Lord and has been a living testimony ever since. Curt is praising the Lord for healing him and giving him strength every day. Another hero is Curt's wife, Beth, who was by his side in the hospital. Beth has helped me on several mission trips and continues to be my partner and helper. Beth's comments are included later in this book. Thanks and love to you both, Curt and Beth!

While we were in the Czech Republic, we were able to take a sightseeing tour of Auschwitz I and II, as well as Birkenau. We had room on the tour bus, so we invited two sixteen-year-old girls from the local village to join us on our trip. One of the girls explained that she wanted to visit the former prison camp because her family history was tied to that location; her grandfather had been killed there.

While we were at the prison camp, we saw twenty thousand pairs of shoes, fifteen thousand suitcases and two tons of human hair. The hair was used for making cloth. We learned that the prison officers would put prisoners into a large room and open a can of cyanide gas. Most of the people would die within ten minutes, or if they were stronger it might take twenty minutes before they died. I was able to take pictures of the familiar tower where the prison trains unloaded people and the barracks that were reportedly set afire when news came out that the war was being lost.

Old communist hideaway.

At this time, in 2001, I began leading mission trips either through my church or for two organizations, Significant Living and Farsight Christian Mission (FCM). Significant Living took over the work of Christian Association of Prime-timers which had been a Christian alternative to AARP. I had worked with CAP and then asked Significant Living to allow me to work within their mission focus. Significant Living is under the umbrella of Total Living Network (TLN). Significant Living is dedicated to helping and providing resources for people ages fifty and older. My job is to give leadership to mission work projects so we can all keep working for the Lord.

Our mission project team from Christ Community Church.

I have seen so many people go on a mission team work project to help others then come home and start volunteering in their own surroundings. Most people who join a mission team are members of Significant Living; many become repeat workers. Usually the work is not too hard physically, and you can work at your own speed. I am seventy-six years old and am having the time of my life. Most participants are in their fifties or sixties, but I will take along any ages eighteen and up. We often work in cooperation with Farsight Christian Mission, which is based in Davie, Florida, and does most of its mission work in the Caribbean. See Levern Halstead's story that follows later.

* * *

Mission
ᴵᴹPOSSIBLE

THE MALENOVICE PROJECT

FRIDAY, FEB. 16- SUNDAY, FEB. 25,2001

" We loved you so much that we were delighted not only to share with you the gospel of God, but our lives as well, because you had become so dear to us"

1 Thessalonians 2:8

This is the old building with the new third story.

Mexico

The first mission trip I led was to Mexico. This is such a rewarding place to serve through our work projects. The first project we worked on was in Acuña, Mexico, south of Del Rio, Texas, where we poured a concrete play area for a children's orphanage. The caretaker at the orphanage was a man named Dennis Carroll. Dennis at one time worked in the United States for a company that sold medical supplies. He gave up his job here to relocate to Mexico. I was able to contact him through a friend of mine who built homes for the poor in Mexico. Dennis later went on to establish a home for young pregnant girls between the ages of thirteen and eighteen. The girls come to this home anytime during their pregnancy. After the baby is delivered, the girls can stay up to a year to learn how to take care of their baby and become a good mother. Most of these girls are still in school, so they finish school while they stay at the home. While they are in class, housemothers watch the babies.

Dennis Carroll has become one of my heroes.

On our second mission trip to Mexico, Dennis had left the orphanage to start the girls' home, so we no longer had an opportunity to stay at the orphanage while we worked. Without our usual place to stay we checked into a local motel and went to the little neighborhood church for Sunday services. We spent time talking to the people there, and one of the ladies remembered me from our trip the year before when we worked on the play area for the orphanage. This lady's name was Bondred Derr. She mentioned she had recently moved to the area. I told her we had just checked in at the local motel. Upon hearing that, she invited us to stay at her home because her mission was to let people on mission trips stay with her. When I asked her how much it would cost to stay at her home, she replied, "Don't spoil my blessing."

We happily returned to the motel and got a refund of our money because we no longer needed to stay there. This allowed us to put that money toward the work project rather than spend it on our housing. We have been staying with Bondred on each trip since then. She is a social worker there. While we have done mission projects, we have also worked a little on the homes of her clients and on Bondred's home where we added a bathroom.

The third hero I met through our work in Mexico is Richard Cobb. Richard was a miserable old man who went with our team from the U.S. to work on a project in Mexico. He seemed to lack guidance in his life and was very unhappy. After he returned home from his first trip with us, he spent the next year thinking about the mission work down there. When it was time to leave on another trip to Mexico the next year, Richard again went with us, but he did not come back. He decided to stay there and help with the mission work. His job was to drive supplies for the girls' home from an overstock warehouse. Companies send all kinds of supplies and gifts that can be of great use to mission projects in that area of Mexico.

Richard is no longer a grumpy old man. He has turned his life around and is helping others turn their lives around as well. For four years he has been as happy as can be since he decided to think about other people instead of himself. To me, this is proof that by helping others you can help yourself. A sad part of this story is that Richard has developed cancer in his hip. He has returned to the Chicago area for treatment, but whenever I call him he is still upbeat and high on the Lord!

Thank you, Dennis, Bondred and Richard.

* * *

Richard Cobb's Story

Harold Jerde asked me if I wanted to go on a mission trip for one week. I asked what it would cost, and he said $450. Wow! To spend $450 on myself to go on a mission trip was a lot in my estimation.

Harold said I could ask for support, but I hated that idea. I was too proud to ask for help—just as I was too selfish to think I would be doing the Lord's work. I also didn't think I deserved a trip to Mexico.

What would my kids think? My family? I was snobbishly poor all my life—no credit cards, nothing expensive in my life. I had a lot of hangups and a lot of baggage of the personal type, having a very fundamentalist background. I'd become a "grumpy old man."

I told Harold I couldn't afford $450 for a mission trip, but I had a van and could carry seven people. He said that would bring down the cost of the car rental, so I went with him to Del Rio, Texas.

We crossed the border to Ciudad Acuña, Mexico, about 8 a.m. Finding La Casa de Esperanza, the orphanage, was an experience of potholes on roads like I had never seen before.

When we arrived at the girls' home, La Puerta de Esperanza, we started our work by building a wall to keep out intruders. The teenage girls needed to be safe from harm and able to sleep and do schoolwork. It was so dangerous that at night they could only go out in groups carrying sticks and stones to beat off wild dogs, rapists, drug dealers and the like.

Dennis Carroll is the director of La Puerta de Esperanza. He spent all of his retirement savings to pay for the cost of the operation. The teenage girls at the home were abandoned by their families.

We grouped together and drove thirty-eight miles to Quemado, Texas, to a warehouse that distributes food, medicine, hospital and office equipment and other supplies to Mexico.

We encountered flash flooding so dangerous we were stopped by the police at three different places and told to go back, but we made it through. I thought it was scary driving in water fourteen inches deep! We had a pretty good-sized bunch of volunteers and unloaded in the rain.

Cornerstone Children's Ranch at Quemado, Texas, helped a lot, and a few local Texas churches did also. The orphanages needed fruit such as bananas, oranges and apples. Fish was almost nonexistent. Dennis had to pay for a housekeeper and a sociologist to teach twelve-year-old to eighteen-year-old girls how to be good mothers. A few of those girls were mentally retarded. It was a very difficult job.

I was a chauffeur for two years from 8 a.m. until 2 p.m. for Dennis so he did not have to be on site from 8 a.m. until 10 p.m.

I had no idea I would stay and spend four-and-a-half years on the border doing His work. I thank God I had the privilege. Even though I now have cancer and have had to return to Chicago, I stay in touch with my friends from Mexico, have true joy in my heart and the Good News on my lips.

My friend Richard, center front.

On another trip to Mexico we went as a team of six to continue work on Bondred Derr's home to make it more usable for workers who stay at her home while working on short-term mission projects. We also wanted to do an outreach in Mexico. Some friends of mine from Elliotte and Wood Excavation gave me a motor home to take with us. We turned it into a motion picture vehicle so we could show *The Jesus Film* and a VeggieTales film for the kids.

On the first night we were to test out our motor home to show a VeggieTales film. We pulled up to a new building that was next to a soccer field. Soon after we began showing the movie, some policemen came out of the building. We had no idea this new building was a police station! They offered to turn the lights off so everyone could see the movie better. We asked them to wait until we could take a few photographs. The movie picture showed up very well on the wall, but our photographs didn't turn out.

While we were there we also trained a few people to make glasses from a kit. This is an inexpensive way of providing glasses for those who need them. I purchase these kits from another of my heroes named Dale Rozell who founded Glasses for Missions. More information on this project will be mentioned later.

Our first showing of the Jesus and VeggieTales films.

Tony, grandson Eric, Harold, Nick, Richard, Tim

This is the motor home the Lord provided for our use in Mexico.

* * *

Costa Rica Trip 1

I would have to say I have left a lot of my heart in Costa Rica and the two main projects we have worked on there. It all got started through another connection of mine, friends who had retired and purchased a farm about three hours south of San Jose. Ruben and Lucy had recently moved there and were thinking of buying some horses and cattle for their farm. I called another friend, Scott Taylor, who had dealt in those types of markets, and asked him to visit them with me. Together, Scott, his wife and I went down for a little scouting trip to investigate opportunities for missions in that area.

During the flight I met a man who lived in the same area of Costa Rica. I mentioned I was interested in doing some mission work in San Isidro. He told me I had to meet a friend of his who had gone to school with him in the United States. Her name was Mary, and she was very well known in that town. We called Mary and arranged a meeting for later that day. She couldn't meet before noon because she was in charge of a Baptist church choir.

When we met her she mentioned that their church's Sunday school buildings were in bad condition because termites were eating the buildings. Because we wanted to help improve the situation we spoke to the pastor of her church and found they had already drawn up plans for a new church building and educational wing and had a price estimate for the project.

We brought a team to Costa Rica, thinking we could quickly put up the new church building. What they had neglected to tell us was the area was in an earthquake zone, so we had much to do to reinforce the foundation to make it safe in case of earthquakes. On the first mission trip our team built a sturdy foundation on reinforced concrete and began constructing the lower portions of the church. We left them with enough money to continue the project and took a team back there the next four years to work. It takes a long time to build a church when we furnish not only the labor but also the money for the building materials.

During our last mission project trip to this area, we were preparing to spend some time in prayer together when the telephone rang. The pastor of the church took the call; it was from a friend who had moved there from the United States. He was a young man named Jimmy and was in San Jose at the time. He was in much distress and told the pastor he was planning to commit suicide. The pastor convinced Jimmy he needed to come talk to him rather than do something so drastic. At the end of the day Jimmy arrived. Hearing Jimmy's story I was again convinced that our purpose in going on these mission trips is not simply to build buildings, but to build into the lives of those people the Lord connects us to in one way or another.

Jimmy told us he had been living with a woman who had taken his money after he cashed his paycheck and then threw him out of the house. We wanted to help meet an immediate need, so we paid for a room for him at the local hotel. Our group was on our way out for dinner, so I asked him if he would have dinner with me. I listened to his story during dinner, and then we went for a walk to get some ice cream.

Jimmy talked about all the bad things he was involved in such as sex, drugs and other mysterious things. The woman he had been living with was not his wife, but his wife was still in the United States.

After listening to him for most of the evening I finally got a chance to talk. I began by asking him a spiritual question: "If you were to die today, where would you be tomorrow?" I've asked that question of a lot of people, and he is the only one to answer, "Hell, probably." I told him the only way out for him would be for him to turn his life over to the Lord. He agreed that was what he should do.

The next morning while our mission team was having devotions by the hotel pool, Jimmy showed up. I told the group Jimmy had expressed a desire to live for the Lord. I then asked a team member, John Smith, to pray for him. Jimmy was with us all week until it was time for us to go home.

Jimmy had lived in New York and retired from AT&T. On September 11, 2001, he was taking the ferry to go into the city that day. He planned to go to the Century 21 building located next to the Twin Towers. Just before the ferry arrived at the dock, the airplane hit the first tower. Didn't God spare your life just in time, Jimmy?

About a month later I telephoned the pastor and in our conversation asked how Jimmy was doing. The pastor said Jimmy was getting his finances straightened out and was trying to get back into relationship with his wife.

As a little side story to our first trip to Costa Rica, when we were looking for mission work to do, I have to tell you about a run-in I had with security at the airport in Chicago on my way down. Ruben and Lucy, my friends who had recently retired to their farm in Costa Rica, asked me to contact their daughter who still lived in the Chicago area to see if she had anything she wanted to send down to them with me. As it turned out, she wanted to send a bag with such items as pictures and mail.

I planned to carry the package on the plane with me, so I put it on the belt at the security checkpoint. Everything stopped! The security police were there, and the Chicago police arrived. We stood there for about five minutes before it became clear what was going on. They pulled my package off the belt and opened it. Along with the pictures and mail, without telling me, the daughter had packed her father's retirement gift from Caterpillar, the company he had worked for. Inside this package were two ten-inch knives in a frame to hang as a decorative piece on the wall. The knives had long silver blades and gold metal handles.

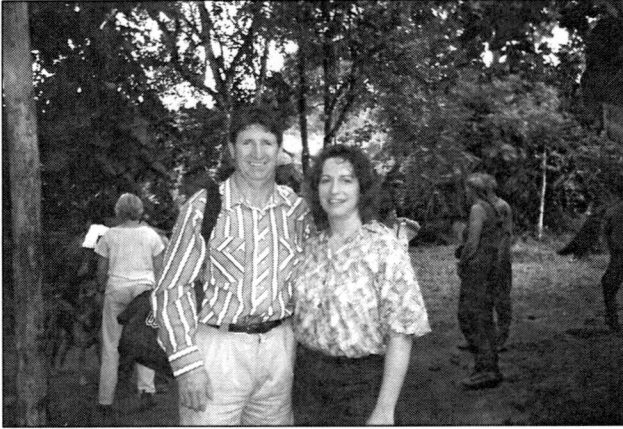

Scott Taylor, his wife and I were the first to go to Costa Rica to find mission work to do.

My first mission team that began work on the church educational building. Mary, our contact person, is in the upper left hand corner.

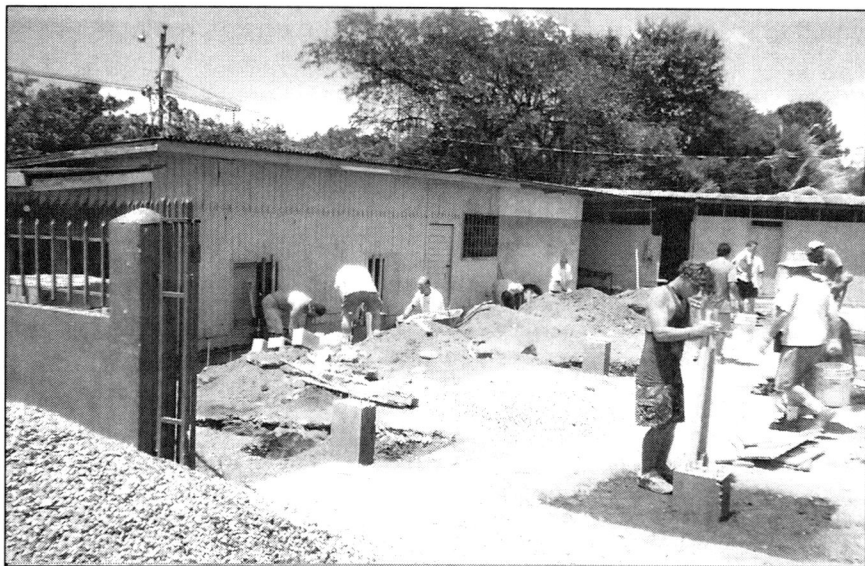

Building under construction.

The police walked over to me to question me and said I couldn't take the knives with me on the airplane; I would have to check them as baggage. I returned to the counter to check this surprise baggage, and the attendant said I had already checked my limit of two bags and could not check any more.

The security police told her that today I would be checking three bags, but by now the plane was boarding and getting ready to take off. There wouldn't be time for me to check another bag. The next thing I knew, they were announcing a delay in our departure; the pilot had suddenly fallen ill, and the plane would be delayed about an hour while they scheduled another pilot for this flight. That gave me enough time to get my third bag checked and loaded.

Now the story doesn't end there. About two weeks after I had returned home from Costa Rica, I received a letter in the mail from the airport security police saying they needed documentation of my story about the knives I had tried to take unknowingly on the plane. I had to send the explanation back to them within fourteen days of the date the letter was written or pay a fine of ten thousand dollars. I needed to contact my friends Ruben and Lucy in Costa Rica, so they could ask Caterpillar for a certified letter stating this package was in fact his retirement gift for his many years of service. The letter had to come from Ruben and Lucy and be sent to Caterpillar then sent to me so I could send it certified to the main security office. I received the letter just two days before the fine had to be paid. Close timing, but it came through. About thirty days later I received a letter saying everything had been taken care of, but I guess my name is still on a list with airport security. See how much fun I have!

Costa Rica Trip 2

The second mission project we took was to build a pavilion for a group of Christian surfers at Jaco Beach. We found out about this project through my friend Levern Halstead, of Farsight Christian Mission. This beach hosted camps for surfers. Hanna and Alex were a couple of missionary surfers who would surf out beyond the breaking waves of the ocean and talk to people about the need to turn their lives around. Hanna and Alex wanted to have a place near the beach camp where they could bring the surfers and continue their spiritual conversations. Alex also taught the Bible to kids who came to the park located next to the beach, and he taught surfing and English classes.

I brought a group of friends to begin building a pavilion for them. While we were there we held a Bible study on the Saturday night during a week of surf camp. Half of those who participated in the Bible study were from the Venezuela surf team that was at Jaco Beach for training. We had to do the Bible study in two languages.

One of our mission team members was a young friend I wasn't sure was saved. He'd said he was saved, but I wasn't convinced he really knew what it meant. About nine of us had a time to get together and talk. The group was made up of my guys on the building team, Alex the missionary, and a friend of Alex who said he was an atheist. A couple of the guys gave their testimonies. The atheist listened but was not seriously interested in what was being said.

It was my young friend's turn to speak. He mentioned he had done a lot of bad things in his life and knew he needed to get away from the group of friends he was hanging out with back at home and make a 180-degree turnaround in his life. Then I knew he understood what being saved was all about.

One of the little side trips we take is a horseback ride up to a large waterfall. We eat breakfast on the way, swim and jump off the falls when we reach them, have lunch and ride our horses back to camp. While we were up by the falls I asked my young friend if he had ever been baptized. He said he hadn't, and his family never even went to church. Well, we baptized him there at the falls that day.

Baptism at the falls.

As we were getting ready to leave for home in the States, all the young guys wanted to stop at a local shop to buy some souvenirs. Most of them bought wooden cross necklaces. My young friend bought one and also bought a large eight-inch wooden cross to put over the door of his dorm room when he got to school at the University of Illinois. It was so everyone who saw it would know where he stood with the Lord.

A couple of times I was able to speak to the young man who was an atheist. During the last conversation I had with him in Costa Rica, he told me he didn't want anything to do with my Christianity. I felt bad, but you can't always say something that will change a person's mind. I returned to the surfers' camp about a year later. Alex, the missionary, asked me if I remembered our atheist friend who didn't want anything to do with Christianity. Alex told me he was now a Christian and was going to school in Denver, Colorado.

Some sad news reached me later in the States. Alex had been riding his bike near the front gate of the surfers' camp and was hit by a car driving past and was killed. Hundreds of people, both Christian and non-Christian, attended his funeral that was held out in the ocean surf. He had taught surfing to so many people and was nearly at a professional skill level himself. I will always remember his challenge to us, as we were heading out to an evening surf contest, to be sure our Christian witness was obvious to all.

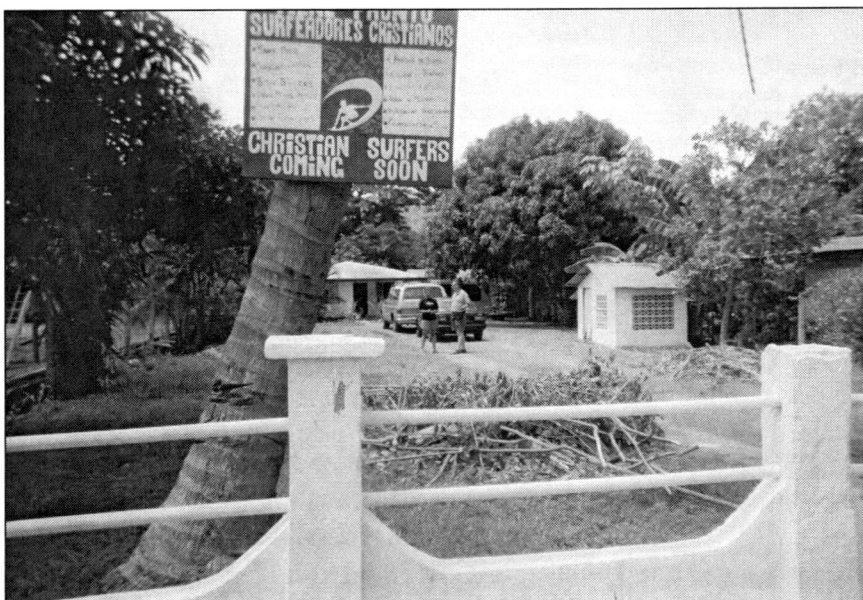

Christian surfers' camp.

Costa Rica Trip 3

I didn't have any immediate plans for another mission trip to Costa Rica when a nineteen-year-old friend mentioned he wanted to get to know Jesus more. We got to talking, and he asked me to tell him about some of the mission trips I had been on. I mentioned he should go with me sometime, and he asked when I was planning to go back to Costa Rica. I told him I didn't have any current plans for a trip. A few days later he called me and said he had two other friends and together the three of them wanted to go with me to a mission project in Costa Rica.

I started thinking about it. Airfare was cheap in the summer, and the kids were on break from school — and when three nineteen-year-old boys want to go on a mission trip, we'd better go. So the four of us went to Costa Rica to help on the church project in progress down there. The boys loved the Christian surfers' camp where we built the pavilion for Bible studies and counseling surfers. The church project is completed now, but they need three more bathrooms. I hope we can go down there soon to get that done. Thanks to my friends Ian, Andrew and J.B.

Costa Rica Trip 4

Recently one of my granddaughters and I visited the church we built in San Isidro to see if we could encourage the congregation to be more intentional about their outreach to their local community. In that location walls are built between all the homes. In the area of the church is a home for the elderly and a children's orphanage. Here in Illinois there is a home for the elderly sitting next door to a children's daycare center. A barn with animals is close by. The elderly residents get to know the children and sometimes take them to visit the animals in the barn. This works out great for everyone.

I wanted to talk to the people in the church about reaching out to the orphanage and to the elderly home in hopes of getting the groups to work together and to grow the church. Allison and I felt our trip was successful. When we talked to the pastor he agreed to mention it to the church congregation, and the church members decided it would be a good idea to try this outreach. Thanks, Allison.

This is Eder from the church in Costa Rica, two ladies from the elderly home, my granddaughter Allison and I.

* * *

Barbados

Barbados is a mission field we also learned about through FCM's ministry. Barbados, a British possession until 1966, is the furthest island to the east in the Caribbean Ocean and is only twelve miles wide and twenty-four miles long. You can travel all the way around the island in one-and-a-half hours. On one side of the island the waves are high enough for surfing, and on the other side the water is smooth as silk. You can be at the beach at 7:30 a.m. to swim and sun yourself. I couldn't get used to driving on the left side of the road there. In Barbados we help at a youth camp that owns a retreat center. Our projects involve making additions to existing buildings and doing building maintenance. The youth camp is overseen by a woman named Crystal and her brother.

Levern Halstead, his wife, Cynthia, Crystal and her brother.

* * *

How Levern Halstead and I met is an interesting story of how God connects us with people who can connect us with other people to help all of us get His work done. After my first trip to Haiti, mentioned earlier, I connected with a brother of a friend from the little Lutheran church where I grew up in the De Kalb area. This friend's brother was an immigration officer at the Miami airport. When we were ready to take our team of twenty-one men down to Haiti to put a second floor on the school building, I contacted this immigration officer and arranged to meet him at the Miami airport on our way down to Haiti. He told me he also goes with another friend to Haiti to work on a church building project they were involved with. The immigration officer and his friend met me at the airport. The friend turned out to be Levern Halstead of Farsight Christian Mission. When our team returned from our project in Haiti, I stayed on an extra day in Florida so we could make plans to join Levern and FCM with a team from Significant Living.

Another connection was that the immigration officer's wife had been a welder in the navy and had recently helped FCM's work in Haiti by welding a bridge they were building in Haiti.

The immigration officer later moved to Alaska and was the person who made the connection for us to participate in an Alaskan mission project for six different trips. I will tell you more on the Haiti and Alaskan projects later. Anyway it seems that each project connection makes another connection to another project and so on. This is how I received another nickname, the connector.

* * *

Haiti Mountain Project

One of the projects we have participated in through FCM involves a church, school and clinic in the mountainous region of Haiti. The bridge the wife of the immigration officer helped weld together made the area more accessible. It spanned about sixty feet over an eighty-foot crevasse. Helpers from fifteen years old and up, including girls, carried four-inch by four-inch angle iron in twenty-foot lengths over a mile to the bridge site. The workers on this project built the bridge on one side of the crevasse. When the bridge had been completely welded together, a hundred people helped pull the bridge into place over the crevasse. That crevasse was very scary to look down into. The new bridge saved the people three to four hours of walking to the church, school and clinic.

Levern had found this remote location and began the ministry there in a tent. Over a five-year period he built the church, nearly finished the school building and was getting ready to build a medical clinic. Our mission teams have come alongside to help construct all three buildings. We have also added an apartment for a doctor and one for a missionary.

FCM has also located a young doctor to work at the clinic. Teresa Murphy is a 110-pound Irishwoman who lives there and sees about fifteen thousand patients a year, doubling as a dentist on Tuesdays pulling teeth. Teresa is another one of my heroes. The missionary was scheduled to arrive soon after we left.

On our first trip up the mountain we were able to take the short road. It was a steep, curvy, narrow dirt road with a drop off of two thousand feet on each side. The road was about nine feet wide. At one spot we found quite a washout, and the truck wheels just matched the width of the road. We also encountered a foot-high ridge in the road that our truck on first try couldn't drive over. We moved most of the passengers to the back of the truck so the front end of the truck was lighter. We were very thankful to make it over the ridge. One of our friends slipped off the truck and had to walk behind us because the mountain was so steep that we couldn't stop the truck to let him get back on. Eventually he caught up to us, and we arrived at the project location together.

We later found out that the next year a hurricane flooded the road and an avalanche of dirt messed it up so badly that the road is now unusable for vehicles and can only be used as a walking trail. The trip we made with our truck took us two-and-a-half hours to get up the mountain. Now it takes six-and-a-half hours to walk up, and one needs to ford rivers.

After we left we were told the doctor was driving a pickup and needed to go through a river. In the middle of the river the current was so strong that the pickup turned over. The doctor got out and was saved, but they lost the truck.

While we were in Haiti, in addition to working on construction projects, we taught a few Haitians how to test vision for those who needed glasses and make glasses from a kit provided by Glasses for Missions. We check their eyes and determine which of twelve available prescription lenses is best for the person who needs glasses. Each kit can provide three hundred pairs of glasses. The frames are made of stainless steel and do not use screws. The glasses cost about thirty-five cents per pair to make. The children learn very quickly and soon can make a pair of glasses in twenty to thirty minutes.

We also use the eye exam as a gospel outreach. When we check their eyes, part of the vision test is to read two spiritual questions: "If you were to die today, where would you be tomorrow?" and "If you were to go to heaven's gate and the Lord asked you, 'Why should I let you into My heaven?' what would you say?" This vision test of spiritual questions is available in many different languages.

Dr. Teresa told us of a young child who had received serious burns when he fell into an open stove. The mother had to walk with him for miles to bring him to the clinic for treatment. After about a year the scar had contracted so much that it drew in his side very tightly. The doctor made arrangements for surgery at Pinion hospital where the child would need to stay for two weeks after the surgery. Rather than stay for the full two weeks the mother and child left the hospital early. By the time they returned home the little boy had so much infection in the burned area that he needed continuous care, and the doctor took him home with her until he could be nursed back to health.

Before a building can be put up, a rock foundation needs to be laid. One way the rocks are collected for the foundation is each child brings a rock with them when they come to school. The children usually carry the rock on their heads. When there is a good-sized pile of rocks, they hire one of the boys to break them into smaller stones for fill or concrete. They say rocks are an important asset in Haiti.

Road building is also a big job in Haiti. If you want a road built, you have to build it yourself, and you need a lot of help to build the road. At one point the Haitians were troubled by snails that were eating their cabbage plants. The snails lived under rocks. The people were encouraged to throw those rocks in the roadway to help build a road for the area. The snails would be a good source of food, but the Haitians don't like to eat them.

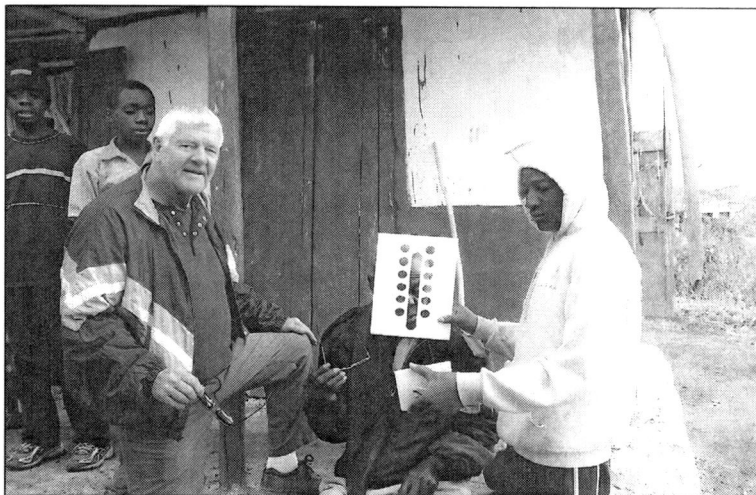

Our first friend to be tested for glasses.

Building the church, school, clinic and apartments.

Children bringing rocks to school for building foundations.

Rocks for the road. Any snails?

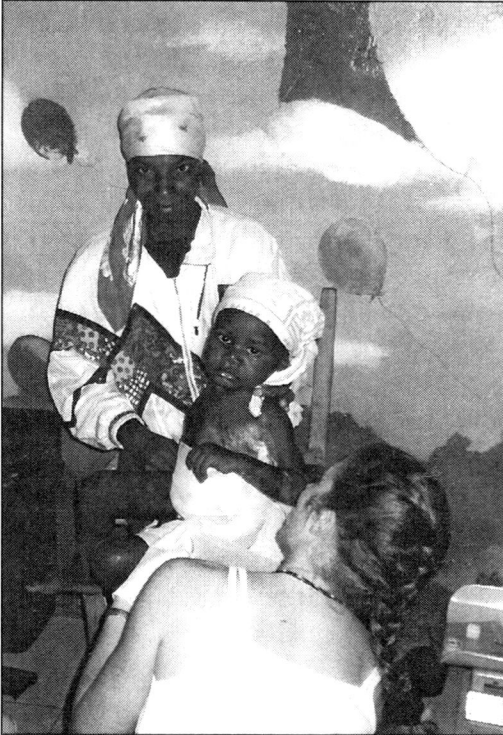

Doctor Teresa caring for a young burn patient.

* * *

A Word About Farsight Christian Mission
by Levern Halstead, founder and director

Farsight Christian Mission was based on the idea of seeing a need beyond our own and doing something about it. Almost from its beginning in 1997 we established a relationship with Harold Jerde and the members of Significant Living.

Twenty years ago a company in the suburbs of Detroit needed an information technology (IT) expert to help them manage their data-tracking needs. The company liked the work I had done on a contract basis so they offered me the position of IT manager. For the next twelve years my family and I lived what we thought was the "American Dream." We had a very good income, great benefits and a nice home in a very nice part of town. In those twelve years the company grew from one computer in one office to two hundred computers in eight offices in five states.

Near the end of these twelve years two things happened. The companies had made some mistakes in their money management and were in financial trouble. At the same time I was re-evaluating the American Dream and searching for some qualities that did not exist. My family and I had begun taking some of my vacation time and leading teams of Christian volunteers on short-term mission trips. On these trips and for a while after a trip I would feel that I had done something worthwhile and meaningful. I had made a difference.

It was after our third mission trip, a trip to Haiti, that I told my wife, "If there was any way I could just quit my job and do this full-time, I would do it." I said this on January 5, 1997.

The companies I worked for needed someone to make them look better on paper than they actually were in real life. I was unwilling to do that, so on January 12, 1997, the company president called me into his office and fired me.

He gave me four months' severance pay, about a year's wages for most. I discovered that in Michigan I could also draw unemployment, so for the next six months I was able to draw three hundred dollars per week.

I literally ran to my office and called my wife to tell her the "good news." We have always been a bit adventurous so we quickly sold both homes in Michigan (American Dream—a home in the city and a home in the country) and decided to start Farsight Christian Mission, an organization that would lead short-term mission teams to help in areas of great need.

We have been based in Davie, Florida, for the past nine years, close to Ft. Lauderdale and Miami airports for easy access to the Caribbean, where most of our work is being done. Fifteen-hundred-plus volunteers have joined us in the work, and several have chosen to take the same leap we did and get involved in full-time work in a foreign country.

Many more details go into our transition—my wife went from homemaker and home business manager to college English professor. We invested my retirement in the work, and even that was strangely like lifting a burden off my shoulders. We now live on twenty-five percent of what I used to make, but every aspect of our lives is better.

* * *

My Trip to Haiti with Harold
by Timothy Z. Sheldon
Circuit Court Judge
Kane County, Illinois

Over the years I had been intrigued with the many stories Harold told of his mission trips to faraway and exotic places. I had just finished reading Rick Warren's book *The Purpose-Driven Life* and was motivated to take a mission trip with Harold. We chose the Caribbean island of Haiti.

I knew Haiti was the poorest nation in the Northern Hemisphere, but I never imagined just how poor.

When we flew in over Port-au Prince, the capital of Haiti, I observed a city of corrugated metal shacks clustered together over acres of land. The close-up views indicated homes that were not as nice as my backyard garden shed.

On the streets (if you were to call them that) the people bustled about by the millions. The people were very busy going and coming. They were all very well dressed and appeared neat and clean. I could not help wonder how they were able to wash and press their clothes and clean themselves without water, sanitation and electricity.

The streets and highways were beyond the imagination of someone from America. The surface of the streets and highways was mud or dirt washed away in many places. Some of the gullies in the streets were several feet deep. The traffic did not stay in any designated lanes. That meant that if the highway was six lanes wide and the majority of the traffic wished to go westbound then all six lanes of traffic went westbound. If one wished to go eastbound on that highway one could choose either shoulder and travel eastbound. If the traffic pattern was equally divided they would choose any lane available to go either eastbound or westbound. Turns in any direction were initiated from any lane. One can only imagine the traffic jams when there are no rules or traffic police.

The streets and highways became even more interesting after we left the largest city and drove up to the mountains. On our way to our destination the highway was intersected by a rapidly flowing river. The truck we were riding in had a winch and cable welded to the front bumper. Our missionary pulled the cable across the river and attached it to a tree. He then activated the winch and pulled the truck across the river to the other side.

The mountain roads were often one lane with a sheer drop off to the valley far below. The roads would wind around the mountain with many blind turns. Our missionary said the secret to navigating the mountain roads was to go fast and use the horn a lot. I am not kidding!

When we arrived at our destination in the mountains, we had to push the truck up the final fifty yards to the dormitory.

Our trip to the mountain complex of our missionary was a breeze compared to our trip down the mountain.

The week we spent at the medical clinic/school/church complex of our missionary was fun and fulfilling. I painted walls of the church and walls in the school. I welded shelves and organized storage rooms in the medical clinic. I played with the many kids in the village and filled them up with pounds of candy I'd brought along. I gave all the clothes I brought with me to the teachers and older school children. You just can't help but love the people.

The week of work went fast, and it was soon time to go down the mountain to leave for home. While we were up in the mountain working, the government of Haiti was fending off a new revolution. The rebel faction was revolting against the government, and the government was attempting to quell the unrest. On the way down the mountain the rebels set cars on fire in the middle of the streets and roamed the neighborhoods with guns. We had to detour through fields and woods in our truck to avoid the rebels. I may have neglected to mention there wasn't enough room in the truck cab for

Harold and me, so we rode outside on the truck bed. A great target for the rebels: two white guys in the middle of Haiti on the outside on a truck bed. At least it was a moving target.

Well, they missed the easy target. In *The Purpose-Driven Life* Rick Warren said God protects those doing His work on mission trips. I prayed that the rebels had read the book.

As one can see, it was a life-changing and memorable trip. I plan to go with Harold on another mission trip. This time, however, I think I'll go with him to Kentucky.

* * *

Haiti, Port-au-Prince

In the area of Port-au-Prince we continue to work on an orphanage and a hospital. On the last trip we made there our team worked on building maintenance, making screens for the windows, and fixed the electrical system. We put eave troughs on the buildings and hooked the troughs up to a cistern for water storage. We also brought twelve sewing machines with us and taught nine girls and two boys from the orphanage how to sew. We brought cloth, needles and thread and other miscellaneous supplies that were needed. The women from our team were encouraged to see how proud the children were of the articles of clothing they made. These sewing skills will be useful their entire lives. We also taught two of the older boys how to do eye exams and make glasses from the kit we left them.

While we were here on our most recent trip we visited a Methodist church where the hospital doctors, Hubert and Junie Morquette, are pastors. After the main service the congregation presented a program just for us on the team. A girls' choir even sang some songs in English. The church wants to give instrumental classical music lessons. Because they do not have enough instruments at this time, we're attempting to collect donated instruments to take them on our next scheduled visit. Instruments can be donated through Farsight Christian Mission.

* * *

The Morquettes' Story
by Annette Schramm

Drs. Hubert and Junie Morquette have a deep and genuine passion for the people of their country, Haiti. Hubert is a surgeon, Methodist pastor and co-founder of King's Hospital in Port-au-Prince, Haiti's capital. Junie is a gynecologist, a Methodist pastor, and the director and, with her husband, co-founder of King's Hospital.

This husband-and-wife team have an incredible medical and social ministry in Haiti. In addition to providing medical attention to the disadvantaged, educating youth on the devastation of AIDS and leadership training, both have been strongly involved in programs for orphans and vulnerable children in their country.

They began their medical profession in the Hospital of Light (Baptist Mission of the South) in Cayes on the southern tip of Haiti. In 1996 they moved to Port-au-Prince to start a private practice, King's Clinic. With the help of the U.S.-based Apostolic Christian Church, the couple started a small maternity ward and hospitalized several patients who could not afford to go to the private hospitals in Port-au-Prince. In November 1996 they leased hospital space and began inpatient and outpatient services at King's Hospital.

In the last ten years more than twenty-five thousand outpatients were served and three hundred Caesarean-sections and one thousand surgeries performed. Five thousand patients have been hospitalized and more than thirty thousand lab tests completed. In the first eight years the hospital served numerous people of the slums of Port-au-Prince, children and pregnant women who would have died if the hospital did not exist for them. Many still testify to the excellent care they received at King's; some even met Jesus as their Lord during their hospitalization. Unfortunately, the last two years of insecurity and unsafe conditions in the vicinity of the hospital due to political unrest have hindered services to the multitude of people in need.

Currently efforts are being made to raise funds to build a new thirty-bed hospital in a safer, more accessible location.

The first phase will be for outpatient services and an operating room with starting costs of $100,000 USD. The second phase at

$275,000 USD will include labs, pharmacy, radiology, sonograms, more operating rooms and an emergency room, along with other long-term care needs, physicians' and nurses' training, plus health programs to benefit the needs of the community.

While working at the hospital as a nurse, Priscille Hyacinthe, Junie's sister, had the vision to start an orphanage, King's Garden. A three-room space was leased behind the hospital, and in the first three years twenty orphans called it home. In 2004 with the help of two American churches the orphanage was moved to a safer, larger location and has grown to thirty resident orphans.

In addition, a school has been built on the property for the King's Garden children and children in the vicinity of the orphanage. For $50 USD per month two children outside the orphanage can receive an education and a hot meal. The King's Garden children are all sponsored by members of Christ Community Church in St. Charles, Illinois. For $50 USD a month the children reside at the Garden with an education and meals. As the children age, vocational scholarships and further education are being considered. Five of the children have been adopted by American families, and five more are in progress.

The Morquettes have hosted missionary groups for more than twenty years. The encouragement and empowerment they receive from these groups is priceless. Haiti is the poorest country in the Western Hemisphere, but it was once considered the Pearl of the Caribbean. Poverty and lack of education due to oppressive dictatorship for most of their two hundred independent years have stripped the country of this title. Yet the people are the warmest and most joyful you will meet anywhere considering their circumstances. They steal your heart. Many missionaries return over and over for that very reason.

Haitian girls' choir.

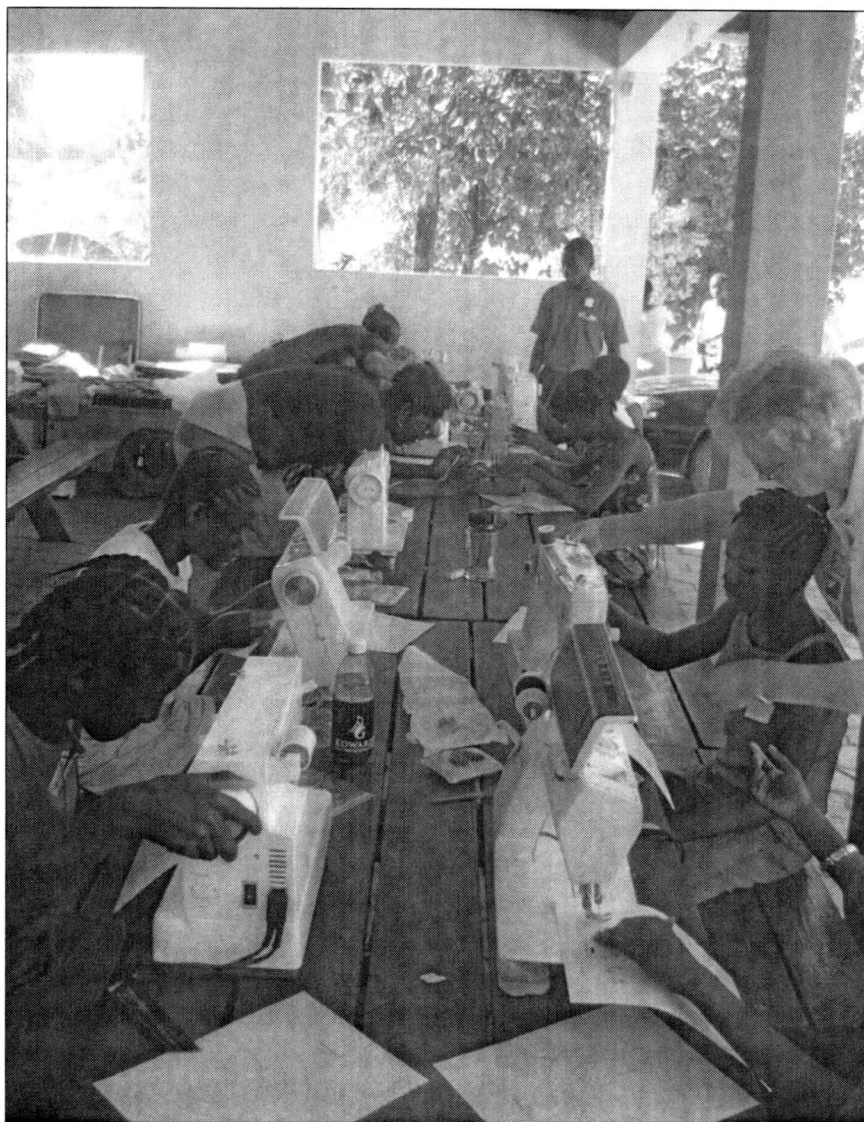

Children learning to sew.

* * *

Partnering with Harold
by Beth Meredith

Harold and I have known each other for more than twenty years. We remember being in a Bible study held in a barn clubhouse during the early years of Christ Community Church. As we learned and grew and served the Lord it became apparent he and I have many of the same passions—to serve others and spread the good news of Christ. I have listened to Harold speak of mission trips for a long time, always being interested in the places and people and seeing God change the lives of those helped and those doing the helping.

While my husband, Curtis, ventured out on a short-term mission trip with our church and Harold before I did, it was this experience that pushed me over the edge to actually go! Viewing the pictures, hearing the stories and watching Curtis glow in the aftermath of new relationships with these "brothers" was all the testimony I needed to know that I too wanted to be a part of something so much bigger than the small sphere of influence I had.

When Harold informed Curtis and me that more people were needed for an upcoming trip to Costa Rica to help build a church, we said yes. The timing was right, the price affordable, and the place would be new. We mixed not only concrete, but also our lives and faith. We enjoyed working, sweating, crying, praising, traveling, eating and sharing our stories with one another to become a family. I learned many things in this foreign land; we don't need to speak the same language to understand love. Smiles and hugs convey a lot. So do screams of pain.

It was at this time that a gallstone decided to present itself to me. The women of the team were with me in the hotel, but none of us spoke Spanish well enough to get me to a doctor. I was thankful the ambulance didn't make it in time, because with God's grace and the prayers of the team the pain passed and left me only fatigued. I was able to rejoin the team for worship at the church that evening!

The next day we rode horses to a beautiful waterfall and took an in-the-back-of-the-truck ride into the jungle for a movie night before continuing with our work. I loved the people, the sights and every moment of the trip (except the pain). I was hooked on mission work!

Next was an early summer trip to Kentucky, with Harold again as leader. I'd heard a lot about this area of Appalachia from previous mission trips he'd been on and from others at our church. I chose this opportunity for my daughter Madeline, who was thirteen then, to experience the camaraderie of team work and the joy of serving. And, since Harold makes every trip fun and exciting with local activities, I knew we would never be bored in a new culture. Being from the Midwest, Appalachia is definitely a different culture.

For this trip our team may have been small — only five of us — but we were mighty. With a supervisor from Christian Appalachian Project (CAP) we helped make a trailer home into a house by adding a front porch, installing vinyl siding, staining doorframes, putting up drywall and insulating. We bonded as a team on the eight-hour drive and continued to become a family as we worked, ate, slept in the same worker's house, held devotions and discussed issues that faced us in this new culture.

Surprisingly, this mission trip was the most difficult for me; I couldn't comprehend the atrocities the local people faced. Weren't we in the USA? Wasn't this just four hundred miles from Chicago? How could these people be so behind the times and seemingly forgotten, being left to fend for themselves? A tour of CAP head-quarters helped me understand their mission and how what they do and the way in which they do it truly make a difference in bettering peoples' lives across Appalachia.

Along with the work comes a little fun. We had an opportunity — because Harold makes the connections — to attend a clogging dance, a bluegrass band's rehearsal, choir practice, Loretta Lynn's child-hood home and a picnic with other CAP volunteers and workers. Traveling with Harold is never all work and no play. Whatever we are doing we are having fun! He is a fly-by-the-seat-of-his-pants, shoot-from-the-hip kind of guy that always lands on his feet — with a huge smile.

Then came Haiti in February 2007. Here again I had heard of and seen pictures of trips to Haiti. I was intrigued by the thought of going to the poorest country in the Western Hemisphere. Whatever I could do to help I was willing to do. Harold assembled a team of nine of us from various parts of the country, one being my mom from St. Louis. This was an answer to prayer.

Our hosts were Drs. Junie and Hubert Morquette, directors of the orphanage. Their house was designed to accommodate groups of missionaries and truly felt like a home away from home. The meals were scrumptious and always interesting. (Even the goat was good!) We did not want for anything and made use of our "family" time at every chance we had. Unity comes easily when you're all in the same situation. We adapted very well to being squished into vehicles and not demanding personal space!

The main thrust of this trip was to teach sewing to the orphans at King's Garden Orphanage in Port-au-Prince. We had two professional seamstresses with us to do the teaching through the use of translators. The twelve sewing machines that were transported to the orphanage were mysteries to the children. They mastered the machines, however, and sewed several different articles of clothing. The hope is for them to learn a skill that will help them through life.

Some small carpentry and electrical work were also part of the plan. I was able to participate in making screens for the windows and got more than enough help from the kids who wanted to learn some basic skills. Actually they were so inquisitive that they used tools in any way they could, that is, drilling into bricks with wood bits, using screwdrivers as drills—they just wanted to experiment on everything! I did say no to drilling into the trees. Future carpenters may have been made in those days.

It was Karnaval (Mardi Gras) when we were there so the children did not have school. I seized the opportunity to be with them individually by giving manicures, pedicures and foot massages. This was primitive at best, but many of the children were eager to have this done. For some it was scary, and they stayed at a distance. Again they loved investigating the tools, using them in any way they could.

Most of the children crave attention and know how to get it by acting goofy or snuggling right up. Some, however, are a bit more difficult to connect with. Writing daily "love notes" and giving hugs and smiles or a soft touch on the shoulder speak volumes to them.

All the children are special, but each team member had a few extra special children attached to them daily. It became routine to know who would be waiting for our arrival and be at our side throughout the day. When it was time to leave it was most painful saying good-bye to these children. Remembering, however, and being grateful for the time we did share made the parting easier. I carry their faces in my heart, correspond with many and pray for them all.

The adventure trip within this trip was a weekend away to Jacmel. It was a delightful four-hour drive through the countryside to the ocean. We visited another orphanage and saw the damage done from a recent hurricane. In the midst of the jungle we saw where the river had widened to three times its original width, taking out the road, the school and a church in the process. We also saw these jungle people bathing and doing laundry in the puddles of river water that was left. To stay at a hotel so nearby while these people lived so primitively was difficult for me to grasp. How can such poverty co-exist with cell phones?

I recommend mission work for everyone and am always eager for the next adventure to begin. I love the travel and discovering different cultures. I also love learning how God can use me, an ordinary woman, to expand His kingdom glory. Individually we can do so much; collectively it is multiplied.

* * *

Trip'n with Harold
by Ro Sparacio

I had always wanted to go on a short-term mission trip to a Third World country. It was my way of feeling good about myself thinking that my works made me acceptable to God. In 1997 I discovered I had it all wrong. I learned we are all made acceptable to God by what His Son Jesus Christ did for every one of us on the cross. I accepted His gift and made Christ my Lord and Savior. I still felt the call to "GO," but my excuse was not having the time. The Lord opened the door when He provided for the sale of my business in 2001. Now I had no excuse and prayed for God to give me an opportunity to serve.

He did so in the way of a conversation with a white-haired, elderly gentleman who asked with a somewhat Southern accent, "How you doin'? Have you ever been on a mission trip?" That was when I met Harold Jerde, and we became good friends. Back then Harold was affectionately known as a "relational giant" because of his passion to serve and share Christ. We began serving together in ministry in our home church, Christ Community Church. We did everything from moving furniture to fixing a leaky faucet. His example about sharing your faith in a bold and respectful way was a lesson well learned.

As our friendship grew, Harold reminded me often about an upcoming STM trip he would be leading with Farsight Christian Mission in Haiti. After asking for some time to pray about it I finally agreed to go. The trip took place in December 2001 and was a seven-day trip with a construction focus in a village in the mountains called Seguin. I didn't even know where Haiti was, let alone Seguin. I found information on the internet about the country, but it was accompanied with U.S. travel warnings that caused me and my wife, Karen, to second-guess my decision. I recalled what someone once told me, "Rarely does God call us to do anything easy." I resolved to go, and Karen agreed this was where He had called me and I must go.

Haiti was once described as the Pearl of the Caribbean. Christopher Columbus is quoted as saying, "What more can man ask for?" when he first laid eyes on the country. Now it is the poorest country in the Western Hemisphere. The sights, sounds and smells are an attack on your senses and are unforgettable. Hurricanes, deforestation and political oppression offer it little hope for change outside of what the Christian church can offer.

Our trip to Seguin was a twelve-hour ride in the back of a pickup truck for most of the team. Once leaving the state highway along the coast we made a hard left into the mountains on roads that deteriorated into not much more than a gravel path. The sights are quite different, and the temperature was cooler as we continued to climb. Small villages and banana, mango and orange trees replaced crowded busy city streets. We stopped for a brown-bag lunch of sandwiches and juice while taking in the beauty of the mountains and a well-deserved break from the jarring ride. We continued on, and as nightfall came the only lights were that of the pickup and an occasional kerosene lamp in a village we would pass through. I began to wonder if our driver was lost and if we would ever arrive. I was thankful the rain held off until we arrived at our destination.

Our first full day was a Sunday, and the team held our own worship service. Communion was planned, but we had to improvise when it was discovered the grape juice was used by our leader (see picture) for his beverage of choice during our lunch stop on the road. We had to get creative as is the norm in Haiti and made do with a mix of grape jelly, water and mashed raisins.

The remaining week we worked alongside fellow Haitians installing a concrete roof on the residence of a U.S. doctor who serves the community most of the year. The interaction with the children became the most memorable experience for the team. As you get to know the people you discover they are content with what little they have. They are a people who are proud of their heritage, are quite creative, work hard and have much to contribute considering their circumstances. The week flew by, and soon we began the journey back to Port-au-Prince.

As we left the village with children chasing us, waving good-bye and asking for sweeties, I reflected on the words of Christ: "The King will answer and say to them, 'Truly I say to you, to the extent that you did it to one of these brothers of Mine, even the least of them, you did it to Me'" (Matthew 25:40). They became crystal clear as feelings of sorrow and joy filled my heart. I felt served more than I had served and already began thinking about my next trip back. My priorities were changed from possessions to people.

As of today I have lost count of my return trips to Haiti, and while each one is memorable in its own special way I have learned "trip counts" are not what matters to God; obedience does. I hope and pray the name of Christ has been magnified and lives have been transformed for eternity by each and every team.

The memory of how I was introduced to a country and people whose needs exceed my capabilities will always stay with me. I am reminded of it every time I get a "'Preciate ya" from Harold. If it were not for his boldness and passion it is quite likely I would still be self-centered on a path of pursuing things that are meaningless.

So I ask you, "Who is the 'Harold' that God has brought across your path, and how will you respond?"

I would like to end with a question I struggled with for a long time, and it may be one you are asking yourself. What difference can one person make in a country that needs so much? This was how someone answered me: "No one can help everybody, but everybody can help someone."

Harold and juice box.

* * *

The following is from a letter written by Gary Schaeffer to Harold regarding how God made Gary aware of a practical need and how God used Gary and others to meet the need for kits to make glasses for the people of Haiti.

*

My wife, Sharon, has been on several medical dental trips to Third World countries and repeatedly has asked me to come along. I thought my spiritual gifts were not best used on the mission field. On Valentine's Day 2004, however, I told her I would go with her on her next trip. In January 2005 we went to Cap Haitian, Haiti, and I was responsible for the sterilization of the dental instruments used. On one of our work days a Haitian lady pointed to her eyes as if to say to me, "Do you have any glasses for me?" Her question never left me, and on the way home from Haiti I decided to go back to Haiti as an optician. (I am a licensed CPA.)

In September 2005, at a Focus on the Family conference for age fifty-plus adults, I prayed I would meet an optometrist. Sure enough, at dinner Friday night Sharon and I met Barb and Roger Rolling from South Carolina. While they had been on a mission trip to Europe they had made glasses. I was floored at how quickly God had answered my prayer request. Barb and Roger connected me with Randy Swanson in Aurora, Illinois, who then connected me with Harold Jerde in the Chicago area. After I explained to Harold over the telephone what I wanted to do, he suggested we meet so he could show me how to make reading glasses.

Even though I live near Seattle, Washington, and Harold lives near Chicago, God intervened by sending a member of my small life group to a conference in Chicago that very same week. God used my friend Gary Whittaker's business trip to Chicago as an opportunity to meet Harold and to learn how to make reading glasses. Then Gary taught me how to make them.

In January 2006, on our next mission trip to Haiti, we took two hundred pairs of reading glasses plus the supplies for making another three hundred pairs. While I was in Haiti, I taught two Haitian Monis, named Harold and Noel Fenaire, how to make the glasses. We continue our contact with both of these men and have now supplied them with another kit to make three hundred additional pairs of reading glasses.

DeAr, My ?riemo Herold ferde

How Are you Im The mame
of Jesus. Thank you for your LeTTer you have sdint
To Me.

This Is reAlly importont To Me I prAy
For you As ThaT CroD blessim of you evevy DAy.
I Think To you My ?riemo. I PdL Lihe seeing You In
Haiti.

Im Happy d you   Write me.

May croD blessimy you ForeVer

      Your ?riemo dodia

      White me bock pLease

      ILoVe you Family Forever

Letter from my friend in Haiti school who is starting to learn
English.

* * *

Jamaica

My first connection in Jamaica was for the purpose of building a trade school there. This project never came to be, but while we were there I met a pastor of a church whose building was rented. This church building was very small and in bad shape structurally. It could not be added on to, so the church decided to purchase some land for building a new church. It took four years to complete the building permit process.

A team of mission workers from Farsight Christian Mission began the project. The workers were staying at the pastor's home. As they were coming in and out, thieves were watching their activities since they realized the team was made up of Americans. When the mission team went off to work on the church one day, the robbers came into the pastor's home, tied up the family and looked for money they thought the Americans would have. Money is now being raised to build a fence around the church area so work on the buildings can continue. From now on, the team will plan to stay at another location so the pastor's family will not fear another robbery.

One day when our team was at Pastor Graham's home the telephone rang. In response to the question, "How are you doing?" the pastor said, "I'm blessed." Isn't this a great answer for anytime we hear this question? Most of us are so blessed.

Pastor Graham and his family. Pastor Graham is an excellent wood-worker and made most of the furniture in his home.

* * *

The Bahamas

Through Significant Living I led a large team of thirty-three people to the Bahamas. We went to work for a Christian organization called Island Encounter founded by Raoul and Karen Armbrister (see story below).

We divided into two groups for our projects. One project was to distribute donations of clothing and other miscellaneous items that would meet the needs of those living in a small village not far away. The other project was to renovate a building Island Encounter was currently renting and planning to purchase. I was told the McDonald's Corporation had also been interested in this property because of its excellent location, but the property owner chose Island Encounter to be the new owner. The building housed a daycare center on the lower level. We worked to remodel the upper level as a restaurant dining hall for weddings. The profit made from the banquet hall would then be used to help fund the meals-on-wheels program for the poor living in the area villages.

***

Missionaries in the Bahamas

Raoul and Karen Armbrister are missionaries and teachers in theology and biblical studies. Raoul answered the call of God and came into ministry from a successful corporate career. He left a six-figure income as well as major investments and has committed his life in service to God. He has experienced the miraculous power of God many times in his life; the most noted by those who know him was his physical healing from being a quadriplegic.

His passion centers on meeting persons at their point of need and building them in areas of gifting and talents that lead from dependence to independence. His programs include woodwork training, carpentry, boat building, leadership training, project development, small business development and spiritual growth.

Karen answered the call after twenty-two years of a successful career as the Bahamas' top television news anchor. To hear her heart is to understand that fulfillment and purpose are greater than success. She is dedicated to teaching and training young girls social graces, sexual purity, etiquette, communication skills and personal development using a program called Metamorphosis. Her Women Empowering Women program takes forgotten and abused women and teaches them sewing and jewelry making as well as entrepreneurial and self-development skills.

Together the Armbristers have developed a feeding and activity center that feeds hundreds daily using hot food and food care packages. They teach and train in the areas of spiritual development, marriage and family, couples' ministry and ministry development. Both are instructors at Access Bible College, where Raoul is the academic dean; they also travel extensively over the USA, building and promoting church partnerships and missions throughout the

Caribbean region. They have built a short-term missions organization, Karazim Ministries, that facilitates churches and organizations in developing mission trips with needed and necessary projects, educational and service opportunities and partnerships that make a difference to all involved.

God is doing a work in the Bahamas through the Armbristers and others with hearts like theirs who are willing to serve.

Adapted from a newsletter; reprinted with permission.

* * *

Alaska

Our mission trips to Alaska have included projects that have been among the most successful during the last seven years I have been leading teams. Remember that my connection with the immigration officer from Florida, who connected me with Levern Halstead from FCM and the work in the Caribbean, later moved to Alaska and made the contact there that we continue to work with. When I called my immigration officer friend after he moved to Alaska, I asked him if he knew of any mission work projects that needed to be done. He told me about a pastor and his wife he had visited on an island three hours away by ferry boat. They had mentioned to him that they had been praying for four years for someone to come up there to help them build a youth camp.

Well, we went to that island for six years, and after the fourth year of building they opened the youth camp we helped construct with mission teams.

The first year we brought a team up to Alaska we helped finish the roof on a two-story lodge building. The lodge contained living quarters for the pastor and family and youth that would come to the camp and was used as a temporary chapel until the permanent chapel could be built. This lodge was made from all rough-sawn lumber and was just beautiful. It was amazing how God provided the lumber for these buildings.

Some man in the area cleared a piece of wooded property for an airport without getting permission from the state government before clearing it. When the state officials found out about it they fined the property owner and told him he would have to donate the lumber to someone. The pastor who had the dream for the youth camp just happened to have a sawmill at the time. So the lumber was donated for this lodge.

After we finished the roof on the lodge we planned to start building the first of two cabins. Each cabin would house twelve people. Unfortunately, when we tried to nail the boards for one of the cabins, the lumber was so wet that water seeped out of the planks. So we had to let the lumber dry out for a year before we could hang the drywall inside. When we came back the second year we finished the first cabin and nearly completed the second. The year after that we finished the inside of the second story of the lodge for living space for the pastor and his family. The following years we built a bathhouse and a permanent chapel above the bathhouse. We also hooked up water, sewer and electric service to the two cabins.

The first year the camp was opened, about a dozen children came, and several lives were changed through Christ. The second year nine more kids' lives were changed as well. What a payoff for hard work! Each of us has felt God call us to this great land so the people may hear of His love and receive it.

One year while we were there, the salmon were running. We had a plentiful supply of halibut and salmon. Now when most people think of Alaska they think of cold snowy weather. Well, on this island, because of the Japanese currents, they have weather much like Seattle's, with more than a hundred inches of rain in a year. One day we were able to go out on the ocean. Another we went shrimping in a small boat like a rowboat to check the traps that were down in four hundred feet of water. We took along a baseball bat just in case a halibut got caught in the trap. Halibut is a large fish. One halibut they caught weighed 350 pounds. They would hit the halibut between the eyes and float it to shore.

Now that our work on the youth camp project is finished we plan to go to Juneau, the capital of Alaska, on our next mission trip to help that same young pastor who has relocated to the Juneau area to plant a church. We expect to work with him on community projects in the location of his church until enough money is raised to put up a building.

I'm including two more stories from Alaska, one written by a member of the team and another from the mother of the pastor who also worked alongside us on the construction projects.

***

A First-Timer's Story
by Debbie Cole

Fourteen Christian Association of Prime-timers (CAP) members gathered on Prince of Wales Island in September 2002 from different parts of the country and walks of life. But we shared a common purpose: to help build a children's camp and retreat center at Hollis Bible Church.

"God called us to Alaska to do a work He had waiting for us to do," said Lore Hoepfner from Wisconsin. "As we worked in the cabins we talked about how the children would hear about Jesus. We came with no expectations—just willing to serve—and we're all going back home changed." Lore was among those on their first mission trip.

Another first-timer, Gerry Kuser, from Maryland, was impressed with how everything "fell into place. The Lord was in it." Used to working on his own, he said, "Everyone joined in and worked together so well. You felt drawn in—you didn't want to stay away. You wanted to be part of it."

Veterans Evelyn and George Dingeldein from Pennsylvania found the unity among team members set this trip apart. "There was openness in sharing, an acceptance and encouragement. Everyone felt included, and we appreciated each one's unique giftedness." They were "blessed by this mission of sharing God's love to Hollis Bible Church."

It was the second mission trip to Alaska for Joyce and Ken Kampenga from Illinois. Joyce liked seeing the project develop since their last visit, and Ken pointed out, "We each had a different job to do. Some cooked, and some hung drywall while others taped, spackled, sanded and painted. The most rewarding work was finishing what we started."

This is the main lodge of the youth camp along with two cabins.

The mission team on the third year of the project.

The mission trip was not all work and no play. The group took time off to tour the island that stretches one hundred fifty miles from top to bottom and serves as home to about five thousand people. Some even hunted for mushrooms in the mossy forests around the church, while others fished for shrimp and crabs.

Fishing was a highlight for Carolyn Wessel, from Michigan, who was experienced in drywalling from other trips and happy to discover some of us could "mud" with the best of 'em.

Work leaders Harold Jerde and Rosario Sparacio, both from Illinois, kept us laughing, and Norm Anderson, also from Illinois, made sure everyone worked as hard as he did. CAP president Roland Johnson found his niche in the kitchen, and Bobbi Denslow from Washington helped the group appreciate our great accommodations with stories of her travels to Third World countries.

"Only the Lord could put together fourteen people from all parts of the country for such an enjoyable week," said first-timer Greg Grenier from Pennsylvania. He described the trip using the hymn "How Great Thou Art," because of "the greatness of the Lord's creation in Alaska" and the "great time we had together as a team."

And what did I, from Florida, also a first-timer, value most? Working with wonderful people to help Alaskan children know God's love—in a spectacular setting of tall, straight evergreen trees, shimmering lakes and misty mountains. On our last day we stood on the ferry gazing back at the island. Suddenly the most beautiful rainbow broke through the clouds and ended close by. Perhaps God was showing us we'd found something better than the mythical pot of gold. It was a lovely gift from Him.

***

The Beginnings of an Alaskan Bible Camp
by Jeanette Reed

In the early 1980s my husband, four sons and I lived in an abandoned shack in Hollis, Alaska, on Prince of Wales Island.

Harold and Jeanette, the pastor's mother who started
the church and camp.

Everything we put on the floor froze in the winter, so during those months we kept our youngest baby in a cardboard box on the table near the wood stove. Sweaters and lots of activity kept the other three boys warm.

We visited our neighbors as often as possible since there wasn't much else to do after dark in Hollis. Being a young Christian mother I was motivated to share the wonderful truth of the gospel, though I often felt very inadequate. We started a little Bible study, and from the beginning I taught children.

One day I realized my children were watching pornographic films at the neighbors'; they had gone over to visit their friends, and the videos were playing. In another instance a gunfight broke out over a stolen bottle of vodka. I was so distressed because my friends did not have enough opportunity to hear and understand the truth.

One afternoon I had a chance to be alone with God. I climbed into an abandoned tree house and poured out my heart to Him. I was sure it wasn't fair for these people not to have a church that could be a witness of the truth. I asked God to give me some land so I could build a church.

Soon after this prayer my youngest son, at one year old, was stricken with a very painful disease. With only antiquated equipment and no specialists, the doctors in our remote area were unable to diagnose the problem, and so for about three months he cried every moment he was awake. Finally social services decided they would cover the cost of taking him to Seattle. Within moments the doctors discovered he had spinal meningitis, and in the first hour we were able to alleviate his pain. He was sent home in a body cast we had to put a hinge on, using duct tape, because he was still in diapers! As soon as this son was stabilized his next older brother was diagnosed with leukemia.

The overwhelming problems and separation were more than their father could endure, and he got a younger woman pregnant, wanted a divorce and left. In the midst of these challenges God answered my prayer for land. Only one homestead was left unclaimed. The doctor who owned it had passed away, and his widow offered to give it to me if I would pay to do the paperwork and fulfill the requirements of homesteading. So this land, about five-and-a-half acres, came to me as the owner and is now where the church and Bible camp are being developed in Hollis.

The young church grew because many neighbors came to help us with my little son, who eventually died from complications of his cancer treatment.

We soon realized there was a very great need for us to give a helping hand to the nearby Native village of Hydaburg. At first the kids could not even listen to a five-minute lesson, primarily because of behavioral issues and an inability to concentrate. We put out prayer books—pamphlets with photographs of the kids and a short description of their personal situations—and asked churches and individuals to concentrate on breaking the spiritual barriers. We had outreaches all over the island doing week-long vacation Bible school programs that were very fruitful. I do not have space here to mention all the young people who have grown up in the Hollis church and gone on to serve God through wonderful Christian lives.

As a result of prayer many people in Hydaburg, old and young, have come to faith in God in recent years. Whole families have been changed in a single moment. My last experience, after twenty years of living on Prince of Wales Island, was giving an invitation to accept Christ in a vacation Bible school class of seventeen children (one was my granddaughter who is saved); the other sixteen all made the decision right there. And God confirmed it the next morning when they told me how they experienced the wonderful feeling of God's Spirit in their hearts as they worshipped Him.

The first camp we held was with children from the village of Hydaburg as well as a few from Hollis. Most of them accepted or grew in Christ while there.

Our hope is that God will let us be part of changing the lives of people through the truth of the gospel. Our new pastor has had his hands full trying to finish up all the building projects required to make that camp usable for a larger number of guests. The ministry to the people of Hollis and outlying communities continues. We give many thanks to the volunteers who have come year after year and have given so much to enable this small group of believers to reach out and share God's truth in ways that are making a big difference in the lives of the people on Prince of Wales Island. Thank you!

* * *

Kentucky, Christian Appalachian Project

A mission trip to Eastern Kentucky is one of the least expensive of all the trips I have led. We go to one of the poorest counties in the United States and work under the supervision of the Christian Appalachian Project organization. Their ministry operates a large variety of human service programs. Most of our work projects are construction projects we find very rewarding.

I've been leading trips to Kentucky since 2003. Now my church has made CAP a ministry partner and sponsors several trips each year, so our ministry to Kentucky has been greatly multiplied. There is usually such a positive response from team members who join these mission trips that now several families make return trips on their own. I have a friend who went with me on eight or nine trips. He recently moved down there to work as a CAP construction supervisor. Another couple who is planning retirement made a one-year commitment to work full-time with CAP to see if God is leading them to Kentucky for the long term.

***

Jack and Lori Scherf's Story

My wife, Lori, and I attended church for many years but were not Christians. We did all the right things—work days, yard work, committees and so on. We never heard about a personal relationship with Jesus.

We church-shopped and found one we liked. Life went on— some of it good, some not so good. Like all parents we had trouble at times. We had a problem on one occasion, and the Holy Spirit told us all we could do was pray. Shortly after that I knew I was not in control of my life and accepted God.

We have put our trust in our Savior. He sent us to Kentucky, and it has been a blessing every day.

A typical mission trip takes about a week. We usually drive down, starting early Sunday morning, and arrive for check-in late Sunday afternoon. Volunteer housing is provided in a dorm-like building. We pack lunches for the following day from supplies provided, watch a safety movie and are on the road to our job sites by 8 a.m. each weekday.

We work on various construction projects in teams of five to eight depending on the type of job we are doing. A CAP employee supervises the project, often assisted by one or two young adult interns. Although each project is different, we often work on houses or trailers that need siding, gutters and soffets, leveling, underpinning, windows, doors, roofs, decks, porches, ramps, plumbing, sewer pipe, indoor drywall and painting. Previous construction experience is not needed. Many workers just learn on the job.

We always find time to talk to the homeowners if they are interested. We want to make sure they know we are there to share the love of Jesus in a practical way. More information can be found about this ministry at the CAP website www.christianapp.org. We also take time to enjoy the beautiful scenery, the good Southern cooking and the bluegrass music of coal country.

***

Tony Pecoraro's Story

I'm really not sure where to begin. It was almost five years ago now, I guess. The church I attended was offering a mission trip to Haiti. After much reflection I finally decided to go. This was the first such venture I had ever taken. The experience was life-changing.

It was only a couple of months after that that I met Harold. There was another trip, this time to Kentucky. It was much closer to home, and thus the preparations were much less involved.

We spent a week in Kentucky putting on a new roof and new siding and repairing drywall on a house. On the last day we had planned to work only a half day. We finished everything we'd wanted to for the week and actually had some time and materials left over.

As it turned out, the couple we were working for had a dog named Otis. Otis was a female pug of sorts. She lived in a pet carrier in the backyard on the side of the hill. The carrier sat on the slope of the hill, and when it rained it would fill with water, so Otis would sit outside and shiver. Since we had the time and materials, we built Otis a doghouse to match the owner's house—same siding and shingles. We put the doghouse up on blocks to level it. When the owner brought Otis over to the doghouse to introduce her to it, I thought he was going to cry. It was all well and good that we had repaired his house; that's what we were there for. But we weren't asked nor did we need to build a house for his dog. He was very moved by the gesture, as were all of us by his gratitude.

It was a couple of years later, on the day after Christmas. Harold had invited me to join him, his grandson and friend, and another friend of Harold's in delivering a just-drivable RV to an acquaintance of his in southeastern Texas, right near the border of Mexico. This was an older RV that needed continual TLC to keep moving. We left the far-western suburbs of Chicago and headed south. Along the way we would stop on the shoulder of the interstate to do some minor tweaking of the engine. We stopped at auto parts stores. We spent one night in the parking lot of a McDonald's in forty-degree weather with no heat. At one point during a night-time leg of the journey, I was under the RV on the shoulder of the interstate in the rain looking for the needle to the carburetor. Every time a tractor-trailer would drive by the RV would rock unnervingly. It took us twenty-four hours to get through Missouri.

Then came the trip to Costa Rica. This was another construction trip. We were to do electrical work on a church being built there. I am a carpenter, not an electrician. But I can take direction. So that was what I did on this trip, followed the instructions of the people who knew what they were doing.

It was exciting for me to visit Costa Rica in that it gave me a chance to resurrect my Spanish skills from decades past. By the end of the ten days I was at least managing some deliberate conversation.

To bring things full circle, the last trip I was on with Harold was to Haiti. He took a group down to teach the children of the orphanage there to sew, the intent being for them to have a marketable skill. He also taught some of them to make reading glasses from a kit that could be another source of income if needed. Harold had been to Haiti some years before, and this was my third time there, so both of us were familiar with the logistics involved. Even after a few visits there, as I have had, it never ceases to amaze me how happy the children generally are. Back home in the States we have so many problems with children being bored, frustrated, dissatisfied. But in Haiti, from what I've seen, the children are happier. In the States we have access to virtually any and everything we could ever want or need. Yet we have depressed youth. In Haiti, comparatively speaking, the prospects are much bleaker. And the children are eager to assist with any project; they seem fascinated by the world around them. Something seems amiss here.

In between my first and latest visit to Haiti, I visited Kentucky maybe a half dozen times on mission trips. Each time I became more enamored with the area, to the point of asking the hard questions. I tell people it can be fun to visit a place for a week; you can have the time of your life. But to live there you have to go to work, pay bills, buy groceries, all that day-to-day ordinary life stuff. So maybe some of the allure gets eroded. But when I asked those questions I couldn't find reason enough to stay away. Now I live in Kentucky, relocated from the Chicago area where I lived my whole life. All I can say is, if Harold hadn't brought me to Kentucky I might not have found the peace I now have. I feel as if I have returned home.

* * *

About four years ago one of our teams was doing rehab work on a mobile home for a young family. As we talked to them and heard their story, we found out the mother had taken in four young abused girls. Their mother had sold them for drugs, so they took them in and are hoping to adopt them. This means nine people are living in the mobile home. Another hero was added to my list, the mother, Regina Carroll. I took such a personal interest in this family that we try to help out in any way we can and have made three trips at Christmastime with special gifts for them.

* * *

The Girls' Story
by Regina Carroll

On June 15, 2004, I received a phone call to come and pick up four of my second cousins. They were at Highlands Regional Medical Center in Prestonsburg, Kentucky. My mother and my oldest daughter rode to the hospital with me. When we arrived a social worker informed me the children had been severely mistreated. She told me of the events the children had endured. I couldn't even believe what I was hearing. The things she explained to me about what happened were horrible. No one should ever be put through that. I was completely shocked.

When I finally got to see the girls, I cried. It was just the thought of what went on that broke my heart. They were so happy to see me. I remember each one of them hugging my neck and smiling. I gladly accepted the social worker's offer. I accepted all four of them into my home. Now for the last four years I have been battling family members in and out of court for custody and rights. They were the ones who didn't want the children then, and now they do in a way— but they don't. All I can ask is for God to give us the strength to go on and to give these children a good life they deserve.

* * *

One Christmas my granddaughter Natalie, who accompanies me on these Christmas trips, and I loaded up a van with clothes, toys and a computer to give to this family. Then we took them on a little trip to Huntington, West Virginia, which is about sixty miles away. We went to Billy Bob's Wonderland and then went shopping. Each girl picked out an outfit; they had never done this before. On our way home I asked the oldest of the four girls how far they had ever been away from home. She said this sixty-mile trip to Huntington was the farthest she had ever gone. Their mother said she thought I knew they had never been out of "the head of the holler" before. Thanks, Natalie, for your help!

Kyle, Chris and Harold.

Natalie and girls.

***

The following story explains much of what God did to connect several people who together filled a need for this family in Kentucky. Both Chris and Kyle drove the van full of love that accompanied Harold and Natalie on their third Christmas trip.

*

A Van Full of Love
by Chris Fisher

"Well, here comes Harold into my life again." That's the first thought that enters my mind when I see the infamous Harold Jerde walking into my coffee shop. Why? Because he has this way about him of getting anyone he meets to do the work of the Lord.

For example, he came into the shop a month ago and sat down for a cup of coffee. I asked him, "What brings you in today, Harold?"

"I need to find a van," he said.

You see, Harold has adopted a family in Kentucky that has quite a tragic tale of abuse and rescue, and he's helped them out for years. Apparently their car died an untimely but overdue death, and the family doesn't have any way to get around without a set of wheels.

Now enter one of Harold's good friends, Kyle Martin. Kyle works at Riverwoods Christian Center in St. Charles, Illinois, with Harold as a maintenance technician, but more important this fella can fix just about anything. If it has wheels he can make it go faster. He's sort of a Tim Taylor kind of guy. I think some golf carts over at Riverwoods can top forty miles per hour, much faster than the recommended factory settings.

Kyle met a friend with a van that wasn't in good working order anymore. As a matter of fact, based on a quick review from a local Firestone dealership, the van would need more than three thousand dollars' worth of repairs to make it roadworthy, from needing new brakes to transmission problems to power-steering issues and more. The owner of the van didn't want to throw any more money into it, so they donated it to the cause Kyle was reluctantly roped into with me because of our love for and affiliation with Harold.

Now Kyle could fix the van, but there were two problems— money and time. The parts needed to repair the van weren't free or cheap. Furthermore, Kyle with his busy schedule at Riverwoods didn't have the time to repair it in the time frame we needed.

Well, Harold excitedly let me know about the van, but it needed some work. I immediately thought of a good friend I'd met through the coffee shop named Frank. Not only is Frank one of the most solid Christian men I have ever had the pleasure of knowing, he's also the owner of Merlin 200,000-mile shops, an auto repair chain in the Midwest. I mentioned to Harold that perhaps we could ask Frank for some help. I called Frank and put him in touch with Harold, and they arranged to meet Kyle at the coffee shop to discuss the need.

We sat down one afternoon, and Kyle pulled out the laundry list of issues Firestone had identified were needed to make the van road-worthy. They talked car talk like two boys in a mechanical candy shop, grunting between descriptions of parts I never knew were on a car. Then came the uncomfortable question: "What are you looking for, Kyle?" asked Frank.

Kyle hesitated. Later he told me he was feeling that we should just shoot high and see where it could go from there. He asked Frank if there was some way we could get those things fixed as soon as possible and somehow get the cost taken care of too.

"We'll take care of it." That's all Frank said.

It was amazing. God is amazing. We just had to get the car delivered to one of the company-owned stores, the nearest one being in Palatine, Illinois.

The next day Kyle transported the van on a flatbed to the repair shop, and they began their work. A couple of days later it was ready to pick up. Kyle picked up the van and drove it home. It was like new. The bill came to just over $3,200, but the bottom line said zero. We were so thankful—thankful to Frank, thankful to the van owner and above all thankful to God.

Now we just needed to get the van down to the family in Kentucky. We had a van that was a van of love, but it was still an empty van. Here comes even more wonderful praise to God. We put out a plea to people we know through our path with God to see if we could get some donations for this family to transform the van into a van full of love.

Harold knows a group of elderly people that meet at church every Thursday for a Bible study. They collected a bunch of food for the family—enough to fill Harold's personal van he was driving down to Kentucky. We received two butchered and frozen deer from Tom, a customer from the coffee shop who donated two hundred dollars for gas and trip expenses. Another guy Harold knows also named Tom, who has been on mission trips with him, donated forty frozen pheasant breasts. Now the van is a Van Full of Love, and Harold along with his granddaughter Natalie can make their third Christmas trip down to Kentucky to this family in need. Praise God for how He works in all of our lives. Harold also wants to thank all the people who donated $1250.00 for trip expenses and money for the family in need.

* * *

The following story was written by Bill Mills, former president of Christian Appalachian Project, the fifteenth largest nonprofit organization in America. Bill was the first to recognize Harold's gifts as a "connector."

*

The first time I met Harold Jerde, he was the leader of a small group from his church participating in a week of home-repair mission work with the organization for which I serve as president, Christian Appalachian Project. Having heard through the grapevine that I was involved in planting a new church here in Eastern Kentucky, Harold sought me out to share his thoughts on church planting.

You can imagine the thoughts that ran through my mind when this retired guy in work clothes appeared at my office to tell me he had some advice to offer. In the moments that followed I learned about a guy who spends most of his time doing mission work— from teaching folks in Third World countries how to manufacture eyeglasses to helping repair homes for the poor in Appalachia. I could tell this was a good man, but I still had my doubts about his motives for hunting me down to tell me what I should be doing with my church.

Harold and I agreed to spend some time together at the evening cookout where his group was having dinner and participating in our volunteer commissioning service. Following dinner and a very worshipful time at the commissioning, a small group of us gathered around Harold to hear his story. He shared his personal walk of faith and the obvious fact that he found real joy later in life when he made Christian service his life's focus.

But Harold's purpose in the discussion was far greater than to share about himself. Rather he was simply building up to discuss one of several key factors in his own renewal process—his church. Harold talked in detail about his church, relating significant details and specific stories about their pastor, the church's relevant music, drama and video programs, and how they can be effectively used to engage seekers and others struggling with life's difficulties. Frankly, he referred repeatedly to some pretty contemporary and forward-thinking church methodologies I was uncomfortable hearing from a guy his age.

Ultimately Harold transitioned to sharing his insights on how our tiny little church plant "should be" endeavoring to reach the masses in our community (like his church does). Spiritually stirred by his passion and experience and at a point where I could no longer with-hold my curiosity, I confronted Harold with this statement: "Harold, I have no idea how old you are, but I would estimate that you are in your seventies (I was thirty-nine at the time). What I do know for sure is that you are way too old to like the things you are suggesting we need to do."

Harold's response is forever etched on my mind as both a call to action and a challenge to never become complacent as a Christian. Harold simply said, "If it brings people to the Lord, I like it."

The words still echo in my mind. They are a challenge for today's church. Essentially they pose a question for each of us to answer—what am I willing to accept in order to lead others to Christ? I know Harold Jerde's answer. "Whatever it takes."

Chapter 3

Stories of People and Principles That Have Impacted My Life

Norm Anderson

Norm has been involved with missions since he was a young man. Growing up in a church that focused on foreign missions he has gone on mission trips and given to missionaries and mission groups for more than forty years.

His interest started with his youth pastor, Jim Fasold. Just out of high school Norm took his first mission trip with his youth group—to work on construction in Kentucky. Then, in the late 1960s, Jim with his wife, Carolyn, faced a year-long challenge of raising funds to go to the mission field with the Greater Europe Mission. Norm gave along with others.

"A year later, while I was stationed with the Naval Air Reserve in Spain, I had an opportunity to visit the Fasolds," he says. "I saw firsthand how they lived and worked to share the gospel." The Fasolds started the Spanish Bible Institute and Seminary some years ago and have now turned over the leadership to the Spanish people under the president, Pedro Sanjaime, but are still available to help.

Norm has traveled with Harold Jerde to Alaska, Haiti, Mexico, Costa Rica and the Appalachian area of Kentucky, and he's been to Africa and the Ukraine. Most of these mission trips have included construction, and he has used his talents cheerfully. One of those talents, he discovered, was not quite up to par with Harold's when they carried cement blocks for building a doctor's apartment in Haiti. He was amazed to see Harold was stronger and more proficient than he was, despite the fact that Norm was younger.

He also recalls a trip he took with Harold and a group into the mountains of Haiti. They stopped their truck for refreshments and pulled out their cooler. Inside were several drinks, including one small container of grape juice, which Harold chose. "We were saving it for communion," Norm says, but later Levern Halstead, another member of the group, mixed up a concoction using raisins.

"I firmly believe in the Great Commission to spread the gospel," he says, "and believe God has given me the ability to help support missionaries with finances. It's still good to go, but sometimes the money can be better utilized for those who are already there."

The last few years he has been working with a church in inner-city missions and has felt God leading him to give there as well.

Whether it is to foreign missions or at home, Norm believes God has called him—through the work ethic his parents taught him, through prayer, through seeing lives changed—to give so others can go to share the good news of hope and faith in Jesus Christ.

* * *

From a Letter by Jerry Rose
President of Significant Living

We at Total Living Network are deeply committed to getting the good news of Christ to the world. We broadcast via SAT-7 to much of the Middle East and North Africa and have also helped launch Christian TV in Romania and continue to provide programming there. We have reached out to orphans, disaster victims and refugees and provided food for the hungry in times of crisis—because serving is the true heart of God.

We also enable our TLN friends to do hands-on missionary work through our Significant Living outreach. One such friend is Harold Jerde. Harold began his missions ministry in his retirement years, when his compassion for the world led him to establish Mission Trips with Harold.

Harold will help people in need on mission trips and at the same time explain the difference God can make in their lives, no matter how poor, lonely or troubled they might be.

Recently, he shared with us about a trip into the Appalachian heartland when he met four little girls who had been trapped in a very abusive home. Harold and his team were able to help them in their new home by adding on two bedrooms and a bath.

Harold views his mission trips as opportunities for Significant Living volunteers to collect memories and have their own lives changed in the process.

We have been thrilled to be part of Harold's great ministry! Many adults in the significant years of life are finding these short-term mission trips to be an ideal way to help those who need the loving touch of Jesus Christ.

* * *

Mission Trips with Harold Touches Lives in Need
by Lynn Tigges

Harold Jerde's memories have been collected from the hearts, the smiles, the tears and the souls he has touched in Alaska, Costa Rica, Barbados, Jamaica, Mexico, the Czech Republic and Kentucky. His ministry began years ago when he set up his first tent meeting. His compassion for the world around him led him to found Mission Trips with Harold, a global-wide ministry that began in his so-called retirement years.

Harold doesn't know how to retire, though, not as long as there is someone else to help in the world.

He has an easy smile, a willing handshake. Even in a world filled with suspicion and misunderstanding, the smile takes him anywhere he wants to go. And the people he meets during his mission trips are much better off simply because he took the time to explain how God can make a difference in their lives, no matter how lonely, how troubled, how poor they might be.

Harold always remembers the man whose life dramatically changed when he introduced him to the Lord. "This man straightened out his life, got married, started going to church regularly and adopted two beautiful Haitian children."

Harold says he only planted the Lord's seed. And what an honor it was to watch that seed grow.

The memory of a mission into the Appalachian heartland still brings tears to his eyes. He points to the picture of four beautiful little girls. . .He could not turn his back on them. . .Life might be hard for them, but never again as hard as it had been.

Harold says, "We had the right people to do the right job on this mission trip. The Lord shows up every time."

He views the mission trips as opportunities for volunteers to collect their own memories and return home with their own stories to tell. The trips can change their lives as well.

One year an angry man went with Harold on a mission to Mexico. Slowly the anger began to subside. "The next year he went again," Harold says, "and he never came back. He has been living in Mexico for the past three years, handing out glasses and showing VeggieTale films out of a motor home equipped with a projector. He is the happiest he has ever been."

Harold has been married to Carol for more than fifty years, and he has three children, seven grandchildren and two great-grandchildren with one on the way.

But his Christian family stretches across many countries and continents. Because of his travels, many Christians and non-Christians alike have a habit of coming up to Harold and asking, "Where have you been?"

He always has a story to tell them.

And with an easy smile and a willing handshake, he sits awhile and shows them the Lord at work.

Adapted from *Significant Living Today* magazine.

* * *

Woman from Spokane

This is a story about a lady from Spokane, Washington, who came to Kentucky to work on a Christian Appalachian Project team when I was on a mission trip there. I went to meet her at the train station in Huntington, West Virginia. During the car ride to Paintsville, Kentucky, she told me her story which made an impact on me as an example of a selfless life even in difficult circumstances. We also made a connection because I had been stationed at Geiger Field in Spokane, Washington, while I was in the air force. This woman mentioned she was married and her husband was in prison near the air force base.

Before she got married, she had been saved and became interested in prison ministry. She began writing to a man in prison, and after she got to know him they fell in love. Because he was due to be released from prison within the next four years they went ahead and got married. They later discovered that even though the law had been changed for new offenders the change did not apply to her husband's sentence. She has been visiting him now for twenty-two years while he serves his sentence for killing a man when he was high on drugs. She is ten years older than her husband and keeps waiting for his release even though they do not know when his term will be over. Now that is a stand-by-your-guy kind of gal!

* * *

Graphology

Years ago I learned graphology, the study of handwriting. I took my first lessons from a priest. He had analyzed handwriting for the court case of Richard Speck, the man who killed eight nurses in Chicago many years ago and died in prison some years later.

I also had a friend named Ira McIntyre who worked as a parole officer for the Kane County Corrections Office in Illinois. He was gifted in graphology. When prisoners were released from jail, their handwriting would be analyzed. Ira could look at a former prisoner's handwriting and say something like, "I think you started using drugs at about fifteen years of age." The person would say, "Who told you that?" His answer would be that he could tell by their handwriting. He could also tell if they had used alcohol, marijuana or cocaine.

I am not as good as my friend Ira, but I have a lot of fun with it and can tell people things about themselves from their past or present. I don't try to tell anything about their future because I believe that would be devilish. I primarily use graphology as a way to connect with people I meet.

Anyway, my friend Ira was a Christian whom I had met through the Christian Association of Prime-timers. He had a battle with leukemia for years and years. Sometimes he would go into the hospital, and the doctors would say, "I don't know if he is going to make it this time." This happened three or four times. Ira didn't let anything stop him from reaching out to serve others regardless of the problems that were a part of his life at the time. He faithfully made phone calls to people he met through CAP, praying with others about their needs.

Finally Ira got to a point where he himself knew he wasn't going to live much longer. I visited him on a Thursday, and Ira told me he was on his last lap.

"Yes, but you're winning!!" I said.

"Yes, I am," he replied. The next Tuesday we attended his funeral.

Thanks, Ira, for reaching out and being faithful to the very end of life!

* * *

Paul Figgins

Another friend I admire is Paul. I call him Hammer. He is a very small man in his eighties, and he just loves to hang out around church, especially since his wife died several years ago.

I first met him when he volunteered to help me set up the children's playground equipment at church. We had to put down a base of two-inch rubber tile that needed to be glued down and then hammered into place. He worked so hard all day long, and that's why I gave him the nickname Hammer.

Paul is known around church as Praying Paul. He has a long list of people he prays for every day. He has had difficult times in his life. His wife died; then his son who was a policeman died of a heart attack while chasing some kids who were causing trouble. Then his daughter-in-law who had recently been widowed was diagnosed with breast cancer only days after she was selected teacher of the year. After that, her home flooded and later burned down. As you can see, he has had considerable difficulty within his immediate family, but he is always "up" and smiling, asking others how he can pray for them.

I just love to be with Paul. Often we go out for brunch after church on Sunday. On a recent typical Sunday I gave him more names of friends to pray for. One of these men is part of a community group of guys from three different churches who are planning to go with me on a mission trip to Kentucky. This friend is having some problems getting over losing his job at General Mills, so we pray for him in our group, and I called on my friend Paul to pray for him too.

Paul is an example of someone who knows, even though he is in an older age bracket, he can have the very important ministry of praying for others. Thanks, Paul!

* * *

Roger Larson

Back when I was building homes I met a friend who did my concrete work. His name was Roger. He had worked hard for another contractor and then bought the business when he returned from Vietnam. I hadn't seen Roger for fifteen years because I relocated my business and our paths never crossed during those years. One Saturday I was at a basketball game at the university in our hometown when a mutual friend told me about Roger being sick with cancer. He was at his home, dying in a hospital bed.

I prayed all weekend about going to see him. I felt God was telling me it was important to visit. I could not go on Monday, and as it turned out Roger wasn't home that day because he was taking a chemotherapy treatment. I did go to see him at 10 a.m. on Tuesday. I knocked and knocked on the door for what seemed like a long time. No one answered. I felt I needed to keep knocking, and finally Roger got up out of bed and opened the door because his wife had gone out on a quick errand.

We talked about small things for a bit, and then we got to talking about the Lord. He mentioned he wasn't much of a churchman. I talked to him about the thief on the cross and said that maybe when we get close to the time when we know our life is short we may think we don't deserve salvation if we have never come to the Lord earlier in our life. I could tell he was getting tired, so before I left I told him I wanted to pray for him. As I was leaving, he said, "You know, when you came to my door today, I knew why you were here!"

When the Lord nudges me to do something I've learned I need to follow through. It is also necessary to talk about the important things of life and death while you still have the chance with people. At Roger's funeral two weeks later his wife told me he sure appreciated me coming to see him just in time! I have hope that I will meet Roger again in heaven someday.

* * *

Dale Rozell

Another friend, whose name is Dale Rozell, is a man I made connections with on a mission trip to Kentucky. Dale has invented and also manufactures eyeglass kits for use on the mission field. His eyeglasses are made out of a stainless steel welding rod with no screws to lose. The glasses come in an assembly kit with enough supplies to make three hundred pairs of reading glasses. Each pair takes only about twenty to thirty minutes to make, and they can choose from twelve different lens prescriptions. I have been able to be his contact person with many of the mission fields we've visited. Some of the kits have gone to Costa Rica, Africa and Islamic people groups. Often if you make a gift for someone, that person appreciates it, and it provides an opportunity to build a relationship—and maybe later you can share about the Lord. Some kits go through Wycliffe Bible Translators. This is a great idea for helping missionaries. You could purchase a kit online at www.GlassesForMissions. org and send it to a missionary out on the mission field. If you click on "History" at this website, you can see the story of how GFMI got started six years ago. To date we know of fifty-two countries where GFMI has been taken.

The following is a list of the biggest customers:

- **SIFAT** (Servants In Faith and Technology) in Alabama. Dale goes there once a year to train pastors, missionaries and lay workers from several different countries. Last year they trained twenty-two workers from twelve different countries. This year they trained sixteen people from eleven different countries, all topnotch, intelligent, hard workers in the kingdom of God.
- **Mission Supply Company** in Australia.
- **Bob Hawk** from Colorado who supplies other missionaries in the medical field.
- **Harold Jerde** from Illinois who promotes, teaches and supplies missionaries and organizes mission trips around the world.
- **Friends of the Disabled S. Car Goes** send mostly to Bolivia and Chile.
- **Don Warren EE International** sends mostly to the Sudan.
- **Pastor Alex Montanano** in the Philippines is using the glasses to open doors in many remote tribes to plant churches—twelve that we know of. He also uses them as an outreach to different people groups, for example, taxi drivers. When he started making the glasses, so many people were coming to his church that they overflowed the huge parking lot and blocked the street.

Dale Rozell writes, "We first met Harold while on a mission trip to Kentucky he had organized. We soon became close friends as we shared our love for Christ and missions. Harold saw the potential for helping many with the GFMI project and has ordered many kits. I am sure one day Jesus will say to Harold, 'Well done, my good and faithful servant.'"

At one time my uncle, Bill Halverson, and my cousin, Dave Halverson, gave me a motor home I wanted to take to Mexico to use in our mission work there. I found out it was going to be too expensive to get the motor home over the border, so it sat in the parking lot of the church for a while. Then God connected me with a ministry that had a need for the motor home.

The ministry, The Word on the Street/Urban Chapel Ministries, was started by a daughter of missionaries from Africa who was a student at Moody. She and another young woman started a ministry for prostitutes on the streets of Chicago. They needed a motor home so they could go into the areas where the prostitutes worked and ask these women to come into the motor home for a cup of coffee. They would speak to these prostitutes and encourage them to stop working the streets. If the girls were interested in trying to straighten out their lives, the Urban Chapel Ministries would help them get into an apartment at no cost for a time while they got straightened out.

It was exciting to see how God used our connections to supply a need for another full-time ministry. The motor home was not used in the way I thought it would be, but God had a bigger and better plan. How great it is to be used of God to fill the needs of others.

* * *

Sheryl Erickson

Another friend of mine by the name of Sheryl went to Kentucky with us on a team from our church a few years ago. On the trip down to Kentucky Sheryl mentioned she had never been on a mission trip before and wasn't sure she could be of use since this was her first mission team experience. Yet she wanted to go and serve even though she thought she didn't have the skills that seemed necessary for the trip.

On this particular trip we were to go into a home and take out the floor all the way down to the dirt. I can still see her down in the dirt,

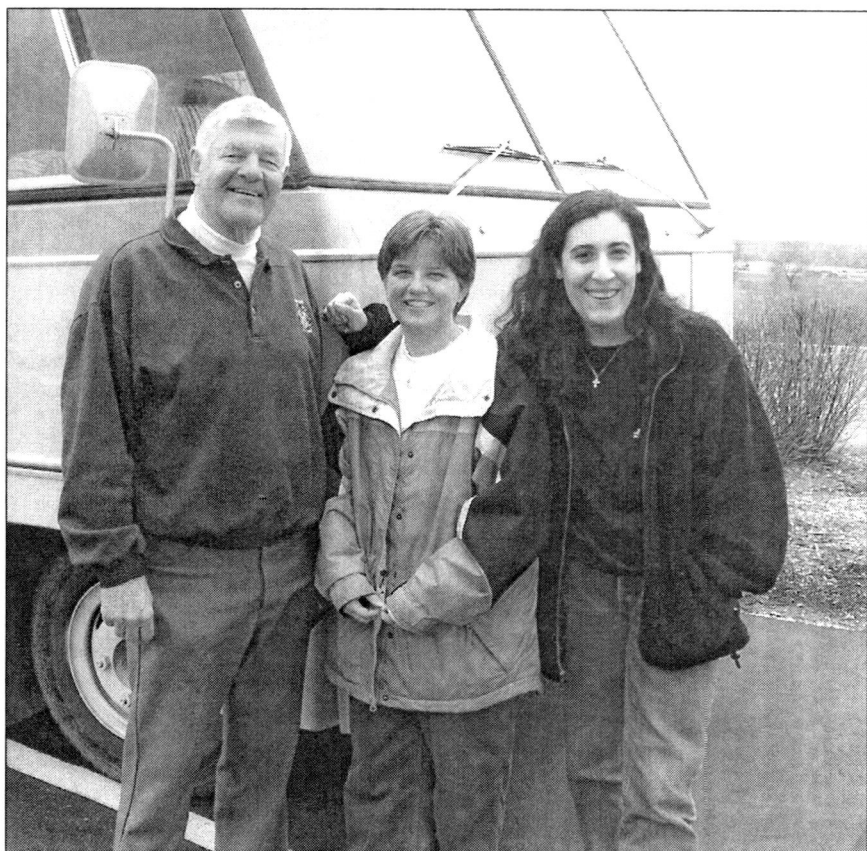

The ladies from Urban Ministries using the motor home.

picking up a dead rat. At break time she would go over to the owner of the home and talk to him about the Lord. He had worked in the coal mines and had black lung disease and other health problems. This man was just taken over by her and the way she presented herself in such a caring, open manner. She didn't feel she had construction skills, but she used the skills she did have to talk to him about the Lord. As I talked to this man's wife, she mentioned that no one had ever been able to speak to him about the Lord. Later, I visited his sister further up in the holler, and she also mentioned his previous lack of openness to the things of the Lord.

When we returned to the Chicago area, I saw a copy of *Chicago Suburban Woman* magazine, and there was a picture of Sheryl on the front cover. The article told how Sheryl was a caregiver for an elderly woman in her community. God had prepared Sheryl with the skills for caring for others, not with construction skills. But a construction project was how the Lord took Sheryl down to Kentucky to serve this man no one had been able to reach for the Lord before then.

The next time I went down to Kentucky I took a copy of this magazine over to the man, and he told me how much he appreciated what Sheryl and our team had done for him. He also stepped out and came twenty miles to visit with the team working there. Sheryl thought she had made a small contribution to this man, but it brought significant changes to his life.

When we make ourselves available and move forward in what God seems to be calling us to do, God uses us as we step out in faith. God accomplishes *His* work in ways that are not necessarily what we think is our work. Thanks, Sheryl!

* * *

Greg Guteman

We are always in a safer and more productive place when we are where we are supposed to be. When God prompts us and calls us to go and serve Him, we must go! I had such a clear calling to go and serve in Sierra Leone last year that going became an act of obedience to go, and any excuse not to go seemed silly. Our focus as a team was multifaceted in reaching out to their needs by visiting schools, inspecting their water filtration, providing and distributing medical supplies, and providing eyeglasses. I don't have any special skill in these areas, the least of them medically (although my wife claims I play a doctor when I self-diagnose myself rather than go see one). So I thought I had an excuse to let this trip pass. I also thought the small business I own couldn't run without me for the duration of the trip, but God said stop this nonsense and go. It's not until we unwrap our clenching fingers from what we think is ours that God gets to do His best work through us.

Our church is in partnership with a church planting ministry in Sierra Leone. The ministry has planted many hundreds of new churches in Sierra Leone and neighboring countries and has reached thousands of unsaved people in recent years. We were going to serve primarily in the village of Bo, where our partner is located, and surrounding villages.

When Harold Jerde heard of our mission he thought it was a great opportunity to start an eyeglass ministry, in addition to the other countries where he has introduced this tangible ministry. A special thanks goes out to Harold for the idea after seeing the dire need for optical help in Sierra Leone.

We were struck by how few people wore glasses, and then after the exams were performed, the strength of prescription needed to help correct the vision. We quickly ran out of the higher strength lens and were trying to accommodate people with what we had. It was especially sad to turn away those with an eye disease whom we were not equipped to help since they needed to see trained doctors.

Our goal was to equip and train the personnel in the health clinic run by our partner, to perform the eye exam and then to fabricate the glasses. This gives them the opportunity to share the gospel and evangelize to the spiritually lost people in these villages. We successfully trained a nurse and three volunteers to perform these duties and are excited to know God's Word is being spread daily to those who need to hear it. It's a warm sight to see the smiling faces of those with new glasses and to think of them going and telling those they meet about what they heard. It's all about multiplication.

The clinic goes on mobile trips to remote villages to administer medical help and now has eyeglass kits added to their offering. On one trip we were able to tag along and experience the outpouring of help they offer. Along with the med distribution we made glasses for what seemed like half of the village. One middle-aged man asked for an eye exam which went well, and we informed him he didn't need glasses; but he insisted, and we mentioned it might damage his eyesight in lieu of helping. Someone reminded us he was the village's chief, and if we didn't accommodate him soon, he could ask us to leave. He was quickly made one of the nicest pairs that day.

Ultimately it's all about God's great commission and reaching others, but I am moved by the relationships we have created with those we are teaching to do this work, relationships that move you to pray daily for their well-being and a hope to visit them again.

* * *

Lacey Hamel

Normal. This is an appropriate word for my upbringing. Middle-class family of five living in a quiet Midwest neighborhood, raised by still-in-love high school sweethearts.

Youth. The greatest thing my parents did was shield me from the harsh realities of our world. I was free to be a child and endure whichever pleasures youthfulness brought.

Curiosity. The catch about transitioning out of childhood into becoming an adult is being curious about the infinite world that exists beyond our reach.

Art. Being an artist and studying the history of art has expanded my knowledge of foreign culture, past and present.

Italy. One of the greatest adventures of my life. Studying and experiencing firsthand the history, values and culture of someone else. I was surrounded by physical beauty. My eyes were opened.

Southeast Asia. Study and pleasure in a new and faraway world. Immersing myself in their world, their life. Poverty hit me hard. The kindheartedness of the locals hit me harder.

Want. I knew what I wanted was to make a difference in this world so the youth could have a chance at a childhood like mine. Free to be young, safe from reality.

Opportunity. I knew what I needed was an opportunity to be involved and begin my lifelong mission to make a change, a differ-ence. To give a better life through education to children; children deserve it.

Harold Jerde. Meeting Harold was not chance; it was destiny. Harold came into my life at the perfect time. At a time when all I had was passion, and all I needed was opportunity. Harold Jerde was my opportunity, and he is that to many.

Haiti. Every element of my past led me to this point. Harold made it reality. I joined forces with Harold and did volunteer work in an orphanage in Port-au-Prince, Haiti. I will take this experience with me forever, and I only hope to touch the lives of those in need as Harold has done for me.

My eyes have seen beauty, and now my heart has too.

* * *

Tom Barry's Story

This story is another example of how God uses people who are connected to each other in one way or another to reach others for Him. It is a story about being obedient to God to go or say whatever He would have you share with those who have a need. God does not always call the gifted speaker to share His message. We can be confident that God sometimes uses common illustrations to draw people to Himself. The Holy Spirit knows just what each person needs to hear.

I have a friend named Tom who is connected to me and my other friend Tony, because Tony's dad taught Tom carpentry skills. Tom and I have kept a friendship over the years. Tom has had some issues in his life that have been hard for him to let go of, but I have tried to encourage him to allow God to lead him in all areas.

One day Tom called me and asked me to come and talk to a friend of his who was very emotionally distressed because of the death of her father. This woman had tried to soothe her pain by taking an overdose of about sixty pills at one time. She had been in the hospital for three days and had just been released when Tom asked me to speak to her about the Lord.

Now I'm not very smart, but I can tell a story! So I went to Tom's house to speak to his friend. I wasn't quite sure what I should say, but the Lord brought to my mind a sermon illustration I had just heard about the walls we build of things that keep us from being ready for eternity. I talked about what might be on the other side of these walls if we would just tear them down. I asked her if Jesus were on the other side of the wall she had built, would she be ready to meet Him when the wall fell down. We talked about how it is necessary to take care of the eternal issues first, and then we can ask the Lord to help us with the other problems we have in our lives. Jesus would help her deal with the loss of her dad.

The woman said she wanted to be sure of her eternity and asked me how to go about it. I encouraged her to confess her sin and receive the Lord's salvation. After we prayed all three of us had tears in our eyes. It is so amazing to see what the power of the Lord can do to draw people to Himself. My friend Tom, who had asked me to come and speak to his friend, also heard the Lord speak to him. He said God was talking to him about choosing to live without those issues he had in his life that kept him from being close to God. I thought I was going just to speak to Tom's friend, but God allowed a two-for-one return that day.

I have spoken to this woman several times since that day encouraging her to live by faith and not by her feelings. She is interested in getting into God's Word, so I passed on some "first steps" and devotional materials and have encouraged other women to include her in a Bible study so she can grow in her faith and dependence on God.

Again it's just one more story of how God uses other people to connect us with someone with a need. He just wants us to be faithful to do the little things we can to point them to the Lord. God can use the words we say or the things we do in serving others to show His love and help bring them to the Lord who can meet their greatest need of Him.

* * *

The following story is by the mother of the former pastor of the church in Hollis, Alaska. We worked with her to build the Bible camp and the new church. It is a story of how God can turn a life around and use it in a mighty way to serve His kingdom.

*

Jeanette Reed's Story

My earliest memory in life was of being attacked by a giant rooster that stuck his claws in the back of my neck, pecked my head and flapped his horrible wings in my face. He terrified me, and I've been eating fried chicken for revenge ever since!

My earliest memory of God was going to a totally fun kids' club when I was seven. The pastor did action stories, made strange noises and jumped up and down; he made us all laugh like cockamamies. I didn't notice the presence of Jesus in my own home, but my maternal grandparents were serious believers.

When I was ten I used to walk miles alone to attend Sunday school because I loved the singing. I don't think anyone loved my singing, but it didn't really matter back then. I had a brief experience going to an old-fashioned Mennonite church. I tried to smile at the babies, and they all started crying. After the service the bus left me behind (I guess they don't like people who scare babies in church). I ran behind it until I thought my lungs would burst. Then someone saw me through the back window. I guess that was when I got good at running. No one my age ever beat me after that until I went to the provincial tournaments when I was twelve. When I came in second I was so miffed that I quit racing altogether until I was a senior in high school.

My father suffered from alcoholism. My mother suffered from narcolepsy and emotional trauma, so I took on a parent's role at a very young age. After my baby brother got hit in the head in a rock war I became a champion rock slinger. I also tied up my sister Susie, left her in an old car at the dump and tried to get twenty dollars in quarters from my parents. Somehow they recognized the printing on my ransom note, and all I got was a good spanking.

I became quite a little boxer, and my dad got some entertainment from watching me box other people's sons. I lost a few of my baby teeth boxing. Once my opponent wanted to collect half of the tooth-fairy money because he knocked out two of my teeth, but I never gave it to him.

As a young teen, my older brother got mixed up with a gang. One of the gang members thought he could abuse my little sister Susie. I knocked him out with one lucky punch, and they never bothered us after that. Another time when I was ten I was at my friend's house. Her father, who was very drunk, was choking her mother. I thought he would kill her, so I knocked him out in one hit, too, with a cast-iron frying pan to the head.

I remember a dear old pastor's wife who had a Bible club in her home, and I really looked forward to attending. All I remember are the Bible stories, cookies and someone who cared. Somehow she was giving me what I needed to help me live through those confusing days. The year my parents divorced, my mother shook and cried so much I thought she would never be all right again. She clung to me and soaked my shoulders with her hot tears.

At thirteen I was buried alive. Facing death helps people remember God. In my distress I screamed out, "O God, my mom! O God, my mom!" Then unconsciousness enveloped me. By that I meant I did not really care if I died, but I wanted God to spare me because if I died it would break my mom's heart. I was miraculously rescued when my older brothers took an off-road shortcut to do some joy riding and saw my feet sticking out of the sand. I should have stuck close with God after that, but I didn't.

My stepfather sent me to confirmation classes when I was fourteen and fifteen. I enjoyed going because ten handsome boys were there and only two other girls. At confirmation we didn't know or care what the lessons were about. I think I was adolescently insane.

In my teens, parties became the big thing. This was where my organizational and social skills came in handy. As president of the students' union I could get lots done. For my sixteenth birthday I organized the biggest dance ever, but it turned into a disaster when my mother nearly got stabbed by a drunk kid.

At sixteen I was unmanageable. My stepfather tricked me into going to a Lutheran youth retreat by arranging a ride for me in a Mercedes with four cute college guys. By flirting on the way, I got a real scary pervert on my trail and so was forced to attend all the Bible meetings to escape from him because he lurked around my hotel day and night. While I was there, God made me aware through the 1 Corinthians 13 passage that He was actually the real author of the Bible. But I did not want to seriously get to know Him because I knew it would infringe on my lifestyle.

At another party my little sister Susie was given way too much alcohol. She went into a coma, and I spent a terrifying night trying to keep her from choking to death in her own vomit.

Those early encounters in the drinking and drugs scene were enough for me. At seventeen I quit.

I moved into the big city and got a job. Soon I had a boyfriend named Bernie as well. One night after he beat me severely I called my parents for help, but my stepfather refused to come. He said I had made my own choices, and now I could live with them. That night I shut my family out of my life, and I was on my own. About a year later I married my boyfriend. Our marriage was rocky, and the abuse continued for five long years. My nose was broken several times. For a while it veered to the left. Later it veered to the right, but the last time it came out straight, so I am thankful for that.

My sister Julie came to know Jesus, and her life was transformed. I think I was hard on her with all my questions, but I wanted to KNOW. She was a wonderful testimony to me.

When I was eight months' pregnant with our second son I drove out to my brother-in-law's to pick up my husband. He was naked in the middle of the living room having sex with some blonde. I stood there with my one-year-old on my hip and my belly swollen with the new child; I felt so strange. I just turned around, shut the door and drove home. I packed up my things and moved out. A few months after the baby was born, my husband and I were reunited amid a lot of promises for a good and sober life.

One night Bernie went into a violent rage and wanted to stab me with a knife. I fled, leaving my babies behind. I quickly locked myself in the car. He was naked, long red hair flying wildly as he tried to bust the windshield with the butt of his knife. When I stepped on the gas he fell off the car, and I accidentally ran over him twice, with the front tires and the back. I was afraid to stop so I drove to my in-laws' home.

Bernie wasn't hurt because the mud on the road was deep and the car small. That night he shot off a gun, missing my son's head by about an inch. A few months later after another bad beating I took my sons and left for good. He tried to get me back by saying he had quit drinking, joined AA and begun going to church. He claimed Jesus had saved him and could make our lives new. I never went back to find out.

One day Bernie picked up a hitchhiker who had a bottle of whiskey, and they got drunk. He dropped the guy off then had a fatal crash. I don't know, to this day, if depression caused him to commit suicide or if it was an accident. The autopsy report said he had enough alcohol in his body to poison him to death. In some ways my life became easier after he perished.

When I had to go into the morgue to identify his dead body I realized he was no longer there, and I wondered where he was. At the funeral my heart felt like a ton of lead frozen in ice. I shed no tears. I felt inhuman, mechanical. I had hated him so much, and now I had no one left to hate, no one to blame.

My mom tried to hook me up with an old widowed farmer, hoping I would settle down, but my dad rescued me. Dad had been in the Salvation Army and had quit drinking. He started taking me to church and AA. At church we had to put on our best face, but at AA we all promised "what you say here, what you do here, when you leave here, let it stay here." So we freely admitted our shortcomings and tried to help each other change. With those ladies who had done unmentionable things I found a kinship, and they helped me admit that my decision to never ever forgive my husband might have led to his death. Admitting this was bittersweet because the guilt did not go away, but it was too late to fix it.

The following year at Christmastime I met a tall, dark, handsome stranger. He was not interested in alcohol, drugs or beating women, and that was good enough for me. After five trips to the courthouse I let him badger me into getting married, even though my parents warned me not to. Then police showed up looking for him, because he was accused of murdering his mother. We felt all alone against the world. He asked me to believe him, and I wanted to help. I was motivated not to fail another human being after what happened to my first husband. Dad went back to the bottle, Mom cried, and I closed them both out of my mind. The little boys and I crossed the border illegally, and for the next few years we ran from the law.

One day in Lincoln City, Oregon, we were surrounded by about twenty police cars. They all had rifles pointed at us, and they arrested my husband. One of them tried to open the back door to get my little boys. I panicked and let him know in no uncertain language he had better not open that car door. Mamas turn into bears when their cubs are threatened. He backed off and sent me "home." I thought I was so tough; they didn't even know I was illegally in the country. But I was all alone, and that stupid old RCMP car was my "home." Hot tears stung my cheeks, but I swallowed them.

We had an old motel room for a few days but soon ran out of money. I had to rock two little boys who were crying from hunger to sleep at night, hoping they wouldn't wake up too soon. Watching them suffer opened my eyes to the fact that I had made the decisions that put them in this predicament. I couldn't talk to my family. I had chosen to ignore God. I was at the place the devil likes to get people. Then Satan sort of freeze-dries them with guilt, shame and blame for the rest of their lives.

It could have happened to me forever, but those two little boys crying finally pushed me past my pride and foolishness to plead for help. I felt deeply ashamed to have to talk to the God I had deliberately turned my back on. I was absolutely certain God would never ever forgive me. But because of my innocent little boys I had to try. I cried to God with every ounce of strength I had. I cannot describe that night with words. Guilt from Bernie's death weighed my soul down to the depths with cement fetters. I felt guilty of murder, guilty of hurting my parents and guilty of ruining my children's lives.

The worst of it was *it was all true*. A wrestling match took place in my soul that night. My fiercely independent nature received a death blow from which it has never recovered. I changed from being unwittingly led by an evil force (and on my way to hell) to being willing to be led by the only true source of love and truth.

I wept and pleaded till the wee hours of the morning. Then exhaustion overtook me, and I fell asleep, soon to be awakened by two hungry boys. Mid-morning a knock came on the door. A pastor and some youth were handing out tracts and inviting people to church. I told him that what we needed was food! So they found us a five-pound can of green beans and a sack of oatmeal. As soon as they closed the door we devoured the whole can of beans in a single sitting. Have you ever eaten plain oatmeal for days on end? It is gross, but we ate every bit for breakfast, lunch and dinner.

The pastor still wanted me to have a tract, and you have to be polite to pastors who feed you when you're starving. He showed me the tract "The Four Spiritual Laws." I was listening with every ounce of my soul. I was anxious to see if I could ever be forgiven.

The facts in that little book had an amazingly good deal for me. No plea-bargaining with God was needed. Jesus had *already paid for all my sin* with His own blood. Jesus suffered for me, and He took my punishment. I was declared *not guilty*. Forever! All I had to do was believe it. There is no better good news available on the face of the earth. I had a free ticket all the way to heaven. Suddenly the whole world turned beautiful. I felt the warmth of love I had never known down in the depths of my soul. Every color seemed to take on a brighter hue. I had peace that I could smell, taste and feel.

Later on I had doubts. This was too good to be true. I decided I would test it out. I said, "God, if this is true, I will go to that pastor's church tomorrow, and if they sing the song 'How Great Thou Art,' then I will know this is real. So the little boys and I went to church. The song was not on the list. The special number lady got up and said, "I know the bulletin has a different song listed, but God put it on my heart to sing 'How Great Thou Art.'" That was my song!

Now this was a really big somber church. When I got up and started yelling because I was so excited, the pastor didn't know how to handle the situation. He obviously was not used to service interruptions, so he sent a couple of serious old deacons to calm me down. I didn't care. I sat down and shut up, but my heart was singing anyway. No one tells hearts what to do. I was so thankful. It seemed impossible that I would ever sin again because I knew how much I had been forgiven. I knew Jesus suffered for me, and I did not ever want to hurt Him again.

And we lived happily ever after—not. That's not true, but it seems like my real life began that day.

My husband was still in jail, my kids were still hungry, but I was not alone. The pastor took me to see the governor and prayed with me before we went in. The pastor told me God was the boss over the governor and not to be afraid; just tell the truth. So I did, and the governor let my husband go. We kept running and were caught a few more times. Each time he went to jail I appealed, and they let him go. Finally we ran to Alaska, the land of few policemen. We realized the law enforcement continued to find us by our car, so we got rid of it. We lived on the ocean and traveled around by boat.

We rarely had running water, electricity or enough food, but we did have two more little boys. When the youngest was only a week old, the long arm of the law found us again. I began to believe that old slogan, "Give me liberty or give me death." I appealed to the governor again, and this time, instead of just letting us go, they decided to help us out. They provided a lawyer for us to take our side against the corrupt system.

From the time I first set foot in Alaska, God started giving me jobs. My first job was to help teach a five-day Bible class. I was about six months old in my Christian life, but when the lady who had been leading the class left she told me to use the old stuff in the church and keep on teaching the kids. So I rescued what I could from the rain and mildew and started in. I had to try to learn the lesson myself before I could teach the kids, so we learned together. We lived in an Indian village, and they loved sending the kids to Sunday school. There were about fifty kids from the ages of four to fourteen. After a couple of years God sent a pastor over to help, and now there is a thriving church in that location.

On Thanksgiving Day 1982, we received an official letter stating that the district attorney who had hounded us for ten years had lost his license to practice law, and my husband was free for the first time in his adult life. We moved out to a place called Hollis. There God gave me lots of jobs to do. I helped out old people, taught kindergarten and preschool, taught Bible lessons and hosted an adult Bible study. We actually had a peaceful happy home. The kids and I were growing in knowing God, and some of our neighbors were getting to know Him too. But I was very concerned about some of my other neighbors.

One day there was a gunfight over a misplaced bottle of vodka, and the lady came begging for help. My husband went down to their house to help her, and they shot at him.

The ratio of men to women in Hollis was about ten to one. One lady was sleeping with about ten different guys, which caused a lot of trouble. One huge guy got mad and hit her in the face so hard both of her eyes popped out of their sockets. We had to get a plane to come and take her to the hospital. Another lady who had a similar problem with men got pregnant. When it was time for the baby to come she locked herself in the bathroom of a neighbor's house and said she would only open the door if I came to deliver the baby. I don't know how the baby lived through the delivery, but she was a cute little girl.

I am telling you this to let you know how much my neighbors needed Jesus. I was so upset we had no church for them. One day I went out to our neighbor Deitmier's abandoned tree house and prayed for God to give me some land so I could build a church.

About that time our baby became gravely ill. He cried every moment he was awake. I got so tired that it became a battle to drag myself out of the grog of sleep to comfort the little fellow. The discs in his spine were degenerating. Because we were so poor we had to wait for welfare medical aid. He cried for three long months until we finally got to the children's hospital in Seattle. Then within hours they identified the problem and stopped the pain. They put Steve in a little body cast and gave him something to stop the deterioration. With a little more medical help he recovered. But while he was still in the body cast we had a car accident and were sued. The day we went to court we found out our next oldest son, Paul, had cancer. While I was back at the children's hospital with Paul, my husband took up with other women.

A medical accident with Paul's chemotherapy burned part of his brain. I had prayed for my son everyday, and now every time we went to the hospital I found I was so very angry at God and expressed it while I was driving down the freeway with my son sleeping in the back seat. The doctor said he was sorry, but the brain would continue to deteriorate from the burn and scar tissue. Why didn't God take care of him? I was so angry I was screaming at Him with all my might. Finally the blinding tears forced me to pull off the road because I couldn't see anymore. (I felt blind in more ways than one.) I sat in the car and smoldered as a dumb radio preacher droned on about what people's names meant.

When Paul was born I expected a girl and had to ask God to give me a name to put on the birth certificate. At the last minute I opened the Bible and found "Paul Josiah." Now this preacher said Paul meant "little one" and Josiah meant "whom God heals." You may not understand my logic, but this was what I thought. It occurred to me that on the day Paul was born God knew he would suffer and need healing, and that was why He gave me the name Paul Josiah. That was enough of a shred of hope for me to forgive God and hang on to faith in him. Not that I had anyone else to turn to anyway, but it comforted me.

One year we lived in a float house in a place where there were more bears than people. That year we bought our son Ron a new bike for his birthday, and he took it out for the first spin. A bear chased him. In Ron's attempt to get away he panicked and made a mistake in judgment. He hit a big rock with his front tire, went flying through the air and landed face first on a boulder. His face was mangled, and the blood was pouring out fast, but he had only a few more feet to run and was able to reach the house. I couldn't stop the blood unless I kept heavy force on it. But I had to go for help, and the camp was a mile away. I told my son Travis to hold the compress on Ron as tight as he could or his brother would die, and I ran to the camp.

The camp cook took us into town. It was Saturday, and the doctor was a Seventh Day Adventist and wanted us to wait a day, but I wasn't taking no for an answer. He did such a poor job stitching Ron up that we had to go back a few days later when the wound burst open again.

Ron was the toughest little boy I ever saw in my life. He never shed a tear over pain, but you could sure set him off if he thought something wasn't fair. Ron was always pleading the case for someone. He wanted everybody to be loved and treated equally. He was often mad at me because he thought I treated my own kids better than I treated strangers. Whenever anyone picked on someone smaller they'd better hope Ron didn't catch them. I often wonder why God made him that way. I guess time will tell.

The brain damage caused Paul to have many grand mal seizures every day and to repeat one sentence over and over like a stuck record. One day we picked up our scariest neighbor. He wore huge dread-locks ten years before they were invented. He lived in a cave, and you would think he was more like an animal than a man. Three adults and four boys squeezed into the front of the pickup. Paul had to sit on Deitmier's knee, and he got his brain stuck on a phrase. For the whole hour-and-a-half drive he said over and over, "Jesus loves you, Deitmier. Jesus loves you, Deitmier. Jesus loves you, Deitmier. Jesus loves you, Deitmier."

When we let Deitmier out of our truck, his eyes were full of tears. "Yeah, I know he does, Paul," he said.

Another time we were on a ship, and a really nasty old man was on board. He was mean to the children and just plain miserable. But Paul's brain damage made it so he could not remember what had just happened, and he kept going back to the man. Finally he crawled up on his knee and gave him a hug. The man's face just kind of trans-formed, and he hugged Paul back and said, "I guess you and me are partners for this trip." And they were. God uses so many things to show us His love.

God used Paul's suffering in many ways. We needed a huge backup of medical help. A lot of the neighbors got their EMT training and took turns helping us. Many of them were more serious with Jesus after their hearts were touched as they helped Paul.

It may seem like a lot of troubles were happening all at once, and they were, but I want to tell you the truth. These problems did not seem very bad at all because I had Jesus with me every second of every day to help me through them all. It was a totally different thing from when the devil had me in the place where I was all alone.

My husband had been terrorized in prison as a young man and was absolutely terrified of being alone. He never came to terms with God over it, and fear drove him to use other women when I was at the hospital with Paul.

One night I had a dream: The whole church was chanting a Bible verse at me. I woke up and looked up the verse. The verse was in the story of Judas betraying Jesus. The moment I read the words, I knew my marriage was over. I also suddenly had a knowledge of where my husband was. I ran down to the road, hitchhiked into town and caught him in the act at Ruth Ann's hotel. He had "fallen in love" with his lover and gotten her pregnant, and he divorced me to marry her. Divorce is something God despises, and so do I. It has a deep paralyzing shame and a stigma within the church that debilitates.

Spiritually I felt as if my foundations had crumbled. Because of the tragedy with my first husband I had gone the extra mile a thousand times in my second marriage. I believed with all my heart that God would do the part I could not do. I felt God had not kept His part of the deal, and I was seriously floundering. I felt unable for God to use me and tainted for life. But I wanted so badly for God to use me to do something worthwhile. I desired to live a life for Him that mattered, but the stain seemed so deep. I felt destroyed.

Emotionally I was a wreck. I lay in my bed without eating or drinking for days. My oldest sons somehow kept the family intact. Travis came to plead with me. I told him I was going to kill myself so he radioed the EMT. I was glad it was my friend Marty on duty. She made me promise not to do anything stupid. Then a pastor and his wife came by. They told me to get up out of bed and sing with them. I learned what the sacrifice of praise was that day. I staked my wavering heart on the God I felt had betrayed me because I had no other place to go. That day I learned the joy of the Lord is my strength.

I felt tossed away like an old used pair of shoes. This betrayal made me want male acceptance. That was bad enough, but there was also the problem of physical cravings; I was used to being married. I was not getting close to anyone; but I enjoyed conversations with any male person. In a frontier place where there were ten men for every woman it was not a safe way to behave, and there were a few fist fights. Then I bumped into a man whose wife had just betrayed him, and the sparks flew; I was living dangerously, and I knew it. I prayed long prayers every night and got up and clung to this unhealthy relationship every day.

After a few months my flirtation bloomed into real temptation. I was miserable, and I did not want to get into sexual sin. I felt that if I were left on my own, sin would reign. I went to a church on our island for help. The Bible study was about David and Bathsheba.

After the service I said, "If you don't pray for me right now, this will happen to me!"

Shortly after that a gunfight broke out between the guy and my friend Suwan. This forced me to end the relationship immediately. (God has mysterious ways to help, even with divorce-crazed women.)

Suwan had moved here from Thailand when he was seventeen. He had been a border guard and had seen a lot of the slaughter done by the Kamarouge in Cambodia. Now in America he spent his time helping out the old people and the single moms in our community. Whenever my car broke he fixed it. He trained my sons in how to use axes and chain saws and do men's work. He came over for supper every night. It seemed like a practical arrangement. I cooked for him, and he did a lot of things I couldn't. He thought he was my bodyguard.

I wanted to know what God's plan was for the rest of my life. The gift of celibacy did not seem to have been given to me, and the Scriptures seemed harsh and unclear. I started going to every pastor I knew and getting their insight. One said this, and another said that. Finally I decided to take a trip to the mainland and see a pastor whom I knew had a doctorate. I thought he would have done more in-depth research.

When I went in, he was very clear on what to do. He said I should stay single the rest of my life. Otherwise if I remarried I would be committing adultery. We talked a bit. Then he said, "I'll just pray for you, and you can go."

When he put his arm around my shoulder to pray his very theologically correct prayer, a mutiny took place within my body. I had all kinds of sexual feelings that were totally inappropriate. I hardly knew him and had no emotional attachment to him whatsoever. The pastor of course had no idea. I just shuddered and prayed for myself in my heart. God knows and sees everything; pastors don't. While the pastor claimed me for celibacy I came to a different conclusion. I decided if my choice was between being considered an adulteress for remarrying and burning with lust, the first was the lesser of two evils. One pastor friend from the island asked me to make a promise—that God would be my best friend and I would not get to know any other men. He said I needed to learn that God supplies all of my needs. So I took his good advice and made a contract with God.

My mom and stepdad bought me an old farm truck and loaned me the money to buy a trailer. They came up two or three times a year to give me some help. They always looked for a guy on the ship whenever they came to visit. He told them about Alaska and sailing all around the world. He kept them entertained on the long ship rides.

I got a job to support my young family, but I hated leaving my handicapped son. Paul needed special care, and I had to pay a lot of my wages for someone to watch him. The caregivers kept my youngest son, Steve, too. He was quiet and easy to look after because he liked to read, write and draw. My ten- and eleven-year-old sons had to fend for themselves. The oldest, Travis, chopped all the wood, kept the fire going and hauled the buckets of water from the creek The next son, Ron, cooked supper for us every night. Ron was an excellent cook. I did dishes to thaw out my frozen hands after I came home from my construction job. Then my two oldest boys got hired by some guy who lived down the way to help build a road. It kept them busy, and I thought it was good because they were being watched by an adult and getting paid for it.

My stepdad came up to check on me, and he was so surprised to find out the guy who hired my kids was the same guy they always talked to on the ship. My stepdad decided to warn this man to stay away from me because I was such a rebel. I think he told every sin I had ever committed, which was quite a long list. But he still hired my kids, so I didn't care. My stepdad also told me that if I wanted an education in what a good man was, my neighbor was the best example.

One time I was trying to help someone get off an addiction to alcohol. Right after we talked he went home, put a shotgun in his mouth and blew his brains out. Other things happened, and I felt helpless to know how to help. So one night I had a big long argument with God.

"Why did You put me here if I can't find the right answers in the Bible to help people when they need help?" I asked.

The man was dead. Why hadn't God helped me find what was needed? I wanted Him to make something happen so I could find the right thing in the Bible whenever I needed to.

The very next morning a lady told me God wanted her to invite me to a place called Prairie Bible Institute for a fall conference. My prayer was answered. God was sending me! On the way I visited with my neighbor on the ship. I realized I was beginning to warm up to him. But I had already had a bellyful of trouble with men, and I had a contract with God.

It was a long three-day trip, and just as we were on the verge of getting there a lady we met said they didn't allow divorced people at Prairie. I was miffed at God for sending me all this way just to show me what I couldn't do. But guess what? That was the year Prairie changed their rules on divorce. So God made a way for me ahead of time.

On my first day on campus at Maxwell Memorial I was awestruck. It seemed to me I had somehow stumbled upon the very people who were continuing the work where the Bible left off. I had never seen or heard anything like it in my life. I stood at the back of the room and sincerely asked God to do whatever He wanted with my life. I was weary to the bone of living with the consequences of sin. I went home with high hopes that God would let me come back.

My neighbor came to talk to me, and right away I told him about my contract with God to stay away from men. He just nodded and went on his way. He never said he was interested, but I wasn't taking any chances. I worked, and the kids kept growing. At Christmastime Paul had a terrible surgery. When we came home all the water pipes in the trailer had frozen and burst. Suwan, my friend from Thailand, came to the rescue. I could never have survived those years without him.

A few months later my friend Marty's husband, Danny, told me about a man who had a homestead but died and left it to his elderly invalid sister. She was not able to fulfill the homestead requirements of the contract. God was answering my prayer for a piece of land to build a church! I sold the trailer, moved into a one-room shack on the homestead where the tidewater came up over the floor. I bought the land, but we still had to homestead it to get the title to it. To help out, my sons started in the construction business when the oldest was twelve.

The man who lived up the street moved his mother to Alaska, and my older sons hauled her water and chopped her wood. They kept asking me to visit her, and we became friends. That friendship made me bump into her sailor son. He was there when we celebrated the Fourth of July. She made fancy cakes, and he brought fireworks for the kids. He accidentally broke my pressure canner when he tried to knock the lid off with a hammer, so he bought me a brand new fancy one. Of course you know I was curious from the start about this man my stepdad said was such a good guy. He seemed all the more appealing because I had to leave him alone, but he never showed the slightest romantic inclination toward me. I prayed God would show me whether I should stay away from Tom or not. I was totally ready to go God's way. I wouldn't dare do my own thing, because I'd had enough of sin's consequences.

The next day Tom asked me for a date! I figured God would show me what to do on the date, which was two weeks away. I prayed every single day. Finally we went out to dinner. I enjoyed the supper. Talking to an adult without my kids was a rare occasion for me. On the way home he stopped at a little park by the ocean. He began to give me a lecture about how hard it was to raise sons without a proper father. Well, I was quite miffed, and I had always been a bit of a scrapper so I staunchly defended myself and told him off! Then he began telling me it seemed I was hardly providing for them since the tide came in over the floor of the house—how healthy was that? But I countered with the facts of their good health and that they were well-adjusted, happy boys in spite of their circumstances.

Then he really got my dander up. "You know what you are?" he said. "You're a homely girl. Yes, homely is what you are."

I was so flabbergasted I didn't know what to say. This guy was really brash, but he had such a serious look. I tried to sort everything around in my mind and make sense of it.

Then he said, "I like homely girls. Homely girls are easier to talk to. You're a homely girl, and I like that."

Well, he had shut me right up. I didn't know what to say. He had just called me homely five times.

Since I had stopped talking he went on to say he wasn't the type to be flirtatious with someone who had four kids, and he didn't have time to waste in silly relationships. He thought I might make a good wife, but if I wasn't serious he didn't want to waste his time. I realized all along he had been trying to tell me he might be a good addition to our family. I decided God had answered my prayer in the affirmative. I said I didn't have a lot of spare time either, but it seemed worth trying to me, and we went home. Later I figured out he meant I was homey—happy at home.

We didn't have any more dates alone. He came over to our house, and we took the kids for walks. He told me the first time in his life he ever felt unconditional love from someone was when Paul took his hand and loved him for no reason. Paul was good at love, and Tom was hooked. To this day I have never figured out if he married me because he loved my kids or if he loved me. But it doesn't really matter.

Our little church homestead project was coming along, and the congregation was growing. Tom helped us build the first cabin with real running water and indoor plumbing. I felt like Cinderella. We had all the food we wanted everyday, and the boys even got real beds with pillows and sheets!! We had kids' clubs three times a week and loved every minute of it. I was able to stay home and care for Paul.

Before we got married, Tom told me he was dreaming of waking up in the morning with me in his arms. I told him, "It's me, four boys, a cat and a huge hairy dog." I was trying to give him some sense of reality. A bachelor doesn't always get it. Little did I know he was about to get a crash course in being Mr. Mom. Six weeks after our wedding Paul was diagnosed with a brain tumor. I had to go to Children's Hospital in Seattle for seven months. Tom took a leave of absence to care for our other three sons. We were also taking care of Isaac, a fifteen-year-old boy whose stepfather was beating him. Isaac's mom asked us to keep him for awhile. Tom and the boys cemented a deep relationship while I was gone, because they needed each other.

After Paul's two brain surgeries we returned home. Make-a-Wish Foundation gave Paul his dying wish. He wanted to go to Thailand with Suwan to see the elephants and monkeys, so we all went. Suwan was such a help, because it seemed the whole country was overrun with tourists. He knew all the places to go and, of course, spoke the language. The things we saw happening to the people were heart-rending. The sex trade of little children was rampant and blatantly advertised.

That fall we sent our oldest son, Travis, who was fifteen, to Bible school. Tom said if he did all right the rest of us could think about going. I felt like Hannah sending Samuel off to live at the temple or Jocabed leaving Moses to the bulrushes and alligators. I wanted some godly men to give my son a good example, so we prayed and let him go.

Paul suffered a lot of pain during the dying process, and it stretched on for months. He finally died on September 25. We were all with him except for Travis. It seemed like everyone came to the funeral. Since we didn't have our own pastor, every pastor from the whole island said something. Then all the people said how Paul blessed their lives, and we all went home. Paul had loved watching loggers cut down trees. His younger brother, Steve, knew of a big stump with roots that looked like big arms to hold him, so we buried him there at the foot of the stump.

I couldn't bear to stay in the church-house alone for even one hour. My heart couldn't take it. So I started putting down the floor joists for the new church. Tom, Suwan and Ron helped when they could, but I did it all day every day through rain, hail, sleet and snow until the roof finally went on. Working on the church in the fresh air was a healing process for me. I did my mourning with a hammer in my hand, and it was good therapy.

Travis didn't let anyone know how much his heart was aching. He decided the Bible school just wasn't serious enough about reaching out to people, so he and a friend decided to go off to a foreign country and preach. They burned their belongings and set out in minus twenty-five-degree weather. No one even knew they were gone. They walked past Linden but got so cold they finally burrowed into a haystack. That night my son staked his life on Jesus and dedicated himself to the mission field. They nearly froze to death. The next day they walked back to the school and never told a soul what they had done. We got him out of that school because we didn't know what he would think of next!

In the fall the whole family went to Prairie Bible Institute. We got a letter in September from the government that said we had money coming from an orphan-and-widow's pension fund that had been accumulating since my first husband died. They asked if we wanted the money. We said, "Sure!" and used it to buy a trailer house next to the school. Now we knew for sure God wanted us there, since He was providing the way.

This Bible school was a very strict place. If you did something wrong they were quick to put it straight. My youngest son had been in a one-room school all his life. He was great friends with his teachers. They always had an individual education plan to challenge him because he had a good mind. Prairie was his first experience in mass-production education.

The first day on the bus some of the kids were calling each other names, and Steve's friend was the butt of the jokes. Steve wanted to defend him, so he yelled at one kid, "Your mom is big, fat and ugly." They all went home, and Steve forgot about it.

The next morning the bus driver gave Steve a slip that meant he was going to get the strap. He was terrified and wondered why none of the other kids received one. When he arrived at school the teacher said, "You are jolly well in trouble now." He sat down at his desk, and the bell rang. A voice came over the intercom telling him to come to the office. With trembling limbs he went. The vice principal was really mad. He told Steve he would get double the punishment, but it would have to wait until the principal returned the next day. Steve was still wondering why no other kids were in trouble. He thought making kids wait for discipline was probably a diabolical adult plan to cause kids to suffer more (from suspense before they had their actual punishment).

Everyone picked on a small boy in the class. I had been encouraging Steve to defend this boy, even if he got picked on himself. That day someone tried to step on the little guy's lunch. Steve saw it and grabbed the offender's leg to divert his effort. The lunch was saved, but the agitator's jogging pants had come down a bit, so a chant went up. "Steve is a pervert; Steve is a pervert."

At recess the chant continued. Steve's friend hit one of them in the face, and then the older brother got involved. Then the playground monitor got involved. Before long Steve was back in the office, and another strapping was added to his list. He had been in trouble with every adult he had met that day.

At the last recess he was going to go and hide, but as he walked out the door a big, fat, ugly woman grabbed him and pushed him up against the lockers. She was extremely irate. Her arms were on either side of him, encircling him. Steve was scared because her bosom was right in his face, and he couldn't get away. (Getting smothered like that would be an embarrassing way for a boy to die.) At that moment I arrived at his school for my physical education class.

Steve let out a strangled cry. "Mom!"

The lady dropped her arms, and he fled right into *my* arms.

My son was in a state of shock and unable to speak. His eyes were as big as saucers, and he couldn't even cry. Even after ten minutes he still couldn't form an audible word. It seems the boy Steve had yelled at on the bus had a rather large and unlovely mother. She had phoned the bus driver, the teacher and the principal and finally came to the school after him herself. After school I had a chat with his teacher, who seemed to agree the punishment had been enough already.

We couldn't come to Bible school every year because we had a little church to take care of at home. My oldest son, Travis, finished his college degree and became the pastor of the church. My second son, Ron, spent time in Bible school and in business school. He lived in the church with a couple of other young men. Both of them were building houses.

In the last few years my time has been divided between work in the church, caring for elderly parents and finishing Bible school. When I met Marlene Adrian from Child Evangelism Fellowship, a lot of my dreams of being really effective in Bible teaching were realized. I have been involved in teaching clubs, training teachers and leading teams in VBS ministry. This has brought me great joy. Because I have watched children suffer I have an impulse to reach them with the gospel and teach them the truth. I am sure it is a gift from God to evangelize. I can feel God at work when I tell other people the truth.

I didn't want the job of looking after my mother-in-law. None of her own children wanted to take care of her because she was so domineering and caused trouble in their marriages. Believe me, she had given me the gears too. In her adult life she managed a lumber company that had interests in several states and provinces. People didn't mess with her. Her children gave her a wide berth—they were teenagers in the sixties, and none of them even tried drugs. That gives you an idea of how tough this gal was.

Because of what is written in 1 Timothy I couldn't find a way to wiggle out of the job of caring for her. So my youngest son was sent to live at Prairie Bible Institute with his older brother—I didn't think he would survive living with his grandmother—and I was imprisoned in her home.

I took my nephew to church one day and complained about my miserable situation the whole way. The service was good. I got ready to go back to my mother-in-law's. As I was leaving I noticed a sign above the door: "You are now entering your mission field." I was struck to the heart as I realized it was true. My present assignment "on the mission field" seemed as if it was in enemy territory. I made up my mind to do my best and to love her.

Suddenly everything changed. She responded to love like water to a dry sponge that had been in the Sahara Desert for years. We began having morning Bible studies. She was just too tough to let me in too close, but one day I saw her watching Billy Graham. When he gave the invitation to be forgiven of sin I saw her bow her head, and I am sure she accepted the Savior. After that we got along famously. When she died, that ministry was a strong testimony to her children and grandchildren. I could never have dreamed up a way to reach them that had such an impact.

A few months later my stepdad died. His daughter had tricked him into changing his will in a way that left my mother destitute. He wanted to change it back and wrote a four-page letter to each of his five children to tell them what a wonderful wife she had been for twenty-five years. He hoped they understood his desire to care for her. The day he wanted to go to the lawyer it snowed several feet.

Then he had a stroke. It was heart-rending to watch him attempt to communicate in half-understood words, trying to get someone to fix the will. He refused food and water and soon died.

Mom was devastated when the stepchildren decided to take everything. She became seriously ill with strange infections deep inside her body. While I was staying with her she told me of the terrible things she had suffered when she went to Bible school. She had been very sick and needed to go home. The people who promised to give her a ride left because she was slow in getting ready. She was delirious with fever and all alone, hitchhiking to the train to ride it home. As soon as she saw her mountains she was sure she would live, and she did. Now I know why my mom loves mountains so much.

Later on she was very sick with a fever again and pregnant with her fourth child. Some Jehovah's Witnesses came to the door, and my dad asked them to take her to the hospital. They dropped her off about a half-mile away during a snowstorm. She trudged her way through, barely able to remain conscious. The baby was delivered at the hospital, and they both struggled to survive. She had been so alone in all of these tragedies. How could I thank God enough that He let me be with her as she faced tragedy again? She was sick for months.

Finally she had to go to the lawyer. She was able to keep her own house and gave the stepchildren the farm and all the oil revenues. She could have kept it all, but she wanted to restore the broken family relationships. Mom did the bravest and most loving thing. She is my hero.

Then my dad's wife left him, and he went into a terrible depression. When I reached his house he was thinking of ending his life. He hates being alone. So God let me stay with him for a few months. We found other people for him to help, and he seemed to find a reason to live again. Some time after that I lived next door to him. At first he was afraid to read the Bible because he thought it turned people into fanatics. By the end of the year he was watching an hour of sermons on TV and reading all our devotionals. He became involved in a Salvation Army church. I knew it wouldn't be long until he needed more care.

The Prairie High School wanted Steve to stay till the end of the year because he had broken a provincial running record. A girl who wasn't good for him was there, and with all these deaths and troubles I didn't want Steve to be alone as Travis had been. I don't think the school ever understood. He finished high school in Alaska, graduating when he was sixteen years old.

Steve enrolled in Northwest Bible College. When they closed their doors he transferred to Prairie Bible Institute, so I came back with him to finish my degree. We lived in the trailer house, and I really enjoyed getting to know this adult son. Sometimes he earned better grades than I did when we were in the same class, but I forgave him.

When I'm at home in Hollis, not one single day goes by that my friend Suwan doesn't come and yell at me for still being in North America when I know and have seen the suffering of other people. He reminds me every day about the statistics, the hopelessness and the fact that he never once heard about Jesus until I told him. He knows exactly how many pastors to people we have here. Then he lets me know that in some places there is one pastor for every million people. To tell the truth, I wish I could spend the rest of my life doing something to change these facts. Right now I am getting ready just in case something wonderful comes up. God might send me on an adventure.

***

Crossroads Church, Alaska
by Travis Reed

Crossroads Church in Juneau, Alaska, began holding its weekly gatherings on January 19, 2008. We meet at the Gastineau Elementary School in Douglas, which is across the bridge from downtown Juneau. Our congregation is made up of a diversity of ages and traditions. We tend to attract twenty-somethings, couples in their forties and young families.

A group of missionaries who have moved to Juneau from around Alaska, the Pacific Northwest and Canada lead the church. My wife,

Jenny, and I are the main church planters, and we moved with our four children to Juneau from Prince of Wales Island in southeastern Alaska.

Our vision is to establish God's kingdom in this community by serving two primary groups: 1) the "urban Alaskan, liberal, environmentalist pagan" is the handle others have used—we see them as "Samarians"; and 2) the young Native families who live in the low-income apartments throughout Douglas. As a result of this demographic we are positioning ourselves to excel in two areas: children's ministry and practical community service initiatives.

We hope to disciple many children through vacation Bible school, AWANA and after-school programs, along with our Saturday gatherings and extra-curricular events.

We aim to promote unity and openness in our community by meeting practical needs through projects such as light maintenance and construction, establishing a community garden, building a recycling depot, organizing an alternative energy co-op, building a community arts warehouse and serving as volunteers in our local festivals and celebrations.

We want to provide positive social alternatives and promote holistic living as a means to build friendships and win our community to Christ.

As we are in the early stages of this missionary project our assets and volunteer force are limited. This is why we are so excited to host missionary teams from around the country who will partner with us to see Juneau and Douglas transformed into a community that brings Yahweh pleasure and experiences the joy of living a life surrendered to Jesus.

As we learn to work together and refine our understanding of our role here in Juneau, we count on your prayers and encouragement to keep our hope and love alive.

Please visit our website at gotocrossroads.org or call me personally if you'd like to get to know us better. We are looking forward to serving with you, learning from you and loving on you.

Travis Reed and family.

Chapter 4

Guiding Biblical Principles

I know my love of ice cream is a vice in my life. One day I went to a favorite ice cream place, Al's Creamery, where I ordered my favorite treat: a chocolate malt. In the entry of this particular Al's Creamery is a kind of library. I saw a book of sayings and quotes. I have always been interested in well-known sayings and quotes, so I looked through this book and found that nearly a third of the quotes were from the Bible. That got me thinking about which quotes were my very favorite, and I came up with three.

I first thought of the story of the woman who had been found in sin. The leaders were going to stone her to death. Jesus walked up and asked what was going on. When the leaders told him they had caught this woman in sin, Jesus replied with a great one-liner: "He that is without sin, let him cast the first stone." What a powerful saying even now. Jesus' example to us is to extend grace. We are all sinners. Through loving others regardless of their need, we can present to them Christ who will meet their spiritual need and extend help to meet the practical needs of others.

The second quote I especially enjoy takes place when Jesus meets a blind man. Jesus took dirt and put it on his eyes, changing his vision to 20/20. Jesus told the man to go and tell no one who had healed him. The man went away, but people followed him and asked him many questions like, "Who is that man? What did He do?" The man who had been blind and was healed by Jesus said, "All I know is, once I was blind, and now I see."

That tells the whole story in one sentence. We are all kind of blind especially when we are in great need either spiritually, emotionally or physically. Just as Jesus changed the blind man's life, Christ can change our lives around from being blind to Him to seeing Him and His work in our lives. We can pass on to others the story of the One who can change their lives, too, at the same time we work in practical ways to meet physical needs.

The third one-liner takes place in the story of Job when his friends came to see him during his time of great trouble. The friends told Job he must be living in sin for all the problems he was having. Even Job's wife told him he didn't know what was going on and he should curse God and die. Job answered, "One thing I know—my Redeemer lives."

What powerful words for today. When we experience extreme difficulties we can always depend on the Lord. Even if we can't see how God is going to work things out at the time or in the future, look back to how faithful God has been in the past and go on firm in your faith in God. Nothing can change the life, death and resurrection of our Redeemer Christ. Those are facts we can always depend on.

* * *

One-Liner Quotes and "Haroldisms"

1. When it is all said and done, there is more said than done.
2. Mud thrown is ground lost.
3. It is easier to stay out of trouble than to get yourself out of trouble.
4. If all you can do is all you can do, then all you can do is enough.
5. I am over the hill, but I am picking up speed.
6. Letting the cat out of the bag is a whole lot easier than putting it back.
7. Good judgment comes from experience, and a lot of that comes from bad judgment.

8. Never miss a good chance to shut up.
9. If you find yourself in a hole stop digging.
10. The quickest way to double your money is to fold it and put it in your pocket.
11. Judge your success by what you had to give up in order to get it.
12. It isn't what you *think* about Jesus; it's what you *know* about Jesus.
13. Loafing is a lost art.
14. Every hero has a sidekick. If you don't feel you're a hero, maybe you're a sidekick.

In addition, I have two favorite songs and a favorite poem that speak about what I believe and have tried to live out through my life.

I'll Go Where You Want Me to Go

Mary Brown   Carrie E. Rounsefell

Sheet music for "I'll Go Where You Want Me to Go."

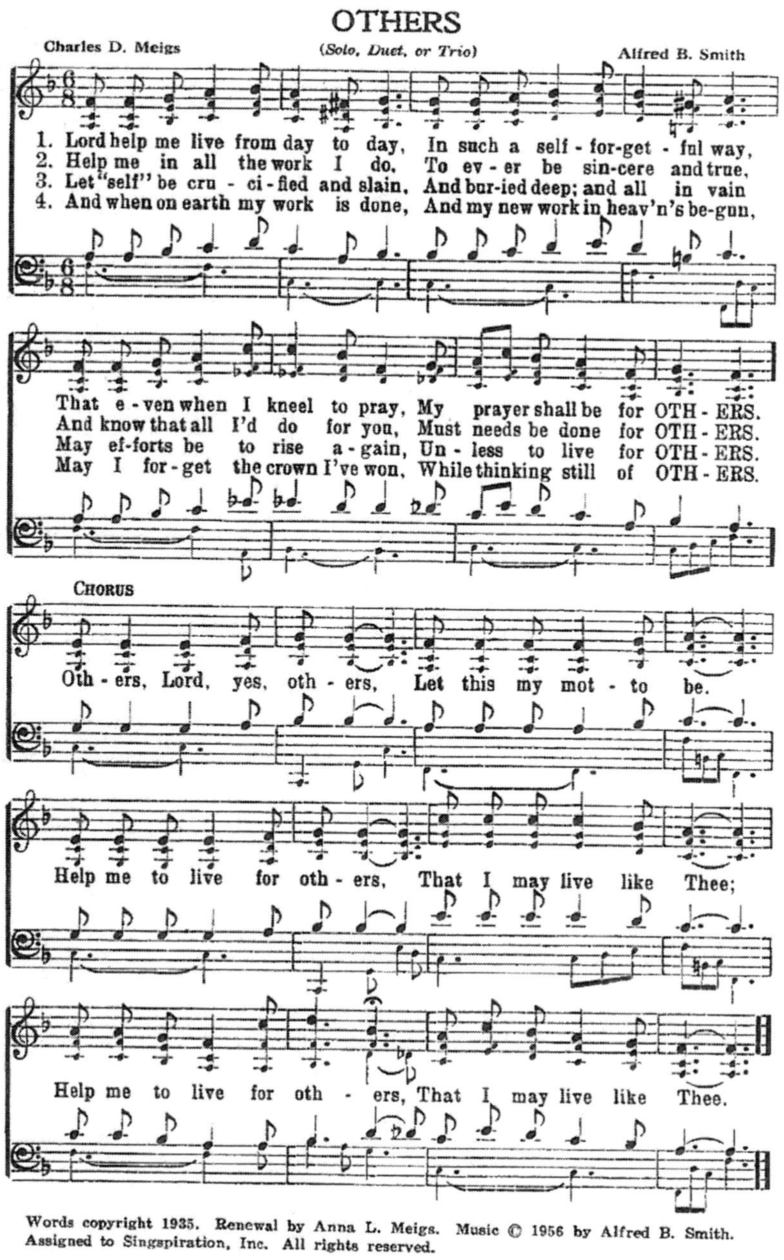

Sheet music for "Others."

I Saw Jesus
by Anonymous

I saw Jesus last week.
He was wearing blue jeans and an old shirt.
He was up at the church building.
He was alone and working hard.
For just a minute he looked a little like one of our members,
But it was Jesus. I could tell by his smile.

I saw Jesus last Sunday.
He was teaching a Bible class.
He didn't talk real loud or use long words,
But you could tell he believed what he said.
For just a minute he looked like my Sunday School teacher,
But it was Jesus. I could tell by his loving voice.

I saw Jesus yesterday.
He was at the hospital visiting a friend who was sick.
They prayed together quietly.
For just a minute he looked like Brother Jones,
But it was Jesus. I could tell by the tears in his eyes.

I saw Jesus this morning.
He was in my kitchen
Making my breakfast and fixing me a special lunch.
For just a minute he looked like my mom,
But it was Jesus. I could feel the love from his heart.

I see Jesus everywhere,
Taking food to the sick,
Welcoming others to his home,
Being friendly to a newcomer.
For just a minute I think he's someone I know,
But it's always Jesus. I can tell by the way he serves.

May someone see Jesus in you today?
The challenge to each of us, who call ourselves Christians,
Is to show to the world that Christ lives in us
By our attitudes and our actions.

Chapter 5

A Day in Beauty

Monday, March 30

It's Monday, March 30, 2009, and the coffee is free at McDonald's on Mondays. The sun is shining, and this is going to be a great day. I came here to Kentucky to finish my book. But today I'm going to forget about that and spend a day enjoying the "lost art of loafing."

I'm headed to Beauty, Kentucky, to see a friend I haven't seen for four years. I met him four years ago when we were working on a lady's home next door for the Christian Appalachian Project. I visited with him that week, and we became good friends. He told me he had worked in the coal mines for thirty-eight years and only went to school to the third grade. School started in August, and in November the teacher left because the river they had to cross was too cold.

He mentioned they were so poor but didn't know it, and I was thinking the same thing, because they keep telling us about being poor all the time. We agreed that us old guys got to live the good years after World War II. He told me he lived on a farm, and they didn't have any money; but they always had food from the garden, meat from the chickens and pigs, and milk from the cows.

Changing the subject he mentioned that when he was a young man and someone on the other side of the mountain got sick everyone went to help out. But now he doesn't even know the people on the other side of the mountain.

I remember we didn't have a car until 1946. All we had was a truck my dad hauled coal in. The whole family would get in the truck—five of us kids and my mother and dad—and we would go to see Gramma and Grandpa on Sundays about five miles away. Now this doesn't sound like a big deal to most of you, but relationships mean a lot more when you are older and you have to work on them. So when you have a friend drive that extra twenty-nine miles one way to see that friend. And if you want friends you have to be one—now. This is the last story in my book about one great day with my friend. We talked, and we laughed until we almost cried. I also got another free cup of coffee at his home. There is nothing like a good visit with a friend on a spring day in Kentucky.

The End

Appendix

Contact information for organizations mentioned in the text

Christian Appalachian Project
P.O. Box. 459
Hagerhill, KY 41222

Christ Community Church
37 W. 100 Bulcom Rd.
St. Charles, IL 60175

Farsight Christian Mission
7128 White Oak Valley Rd.
McDonald, TN 37353

King's Garden
61st Ave. Martin Luther King
Port-au-Prince, Haiti

Significant Living
2880 Vision Court
Aurora, IL 60506

Total Living Network
2880 Vision Court
Aurora, IL 60506

CPSIA information can be obtained at www.ICGtesting.com
Printed in the USA
LVOW11s2301090316

478530LV00001B/110/P